CREATING WEALTH

THE SECRET CODE OF SUCCESS IN THE AI AGE & TIMELESS WISDOM

A PERIODICAL FOR SOCIAL MEDIA & CONTENT CREATORS

A TRANSFORMATIONAL GUIDE TO BUILD BRAND, AND INCREASE INCOME, INFLUENCE, AND IMPACT

Special __FREE__ Bonus Gift for You
To help you to achieve more success, there are
FREE BONUS RESOURCES for you at:

YouTube.com/@newpowerart

- 3+ in-depth training video series on success in music, millionaire top achievers attract more opportunities, achieve more goals and create more abundance

CHUNTIANLE (NEW POWER ART)

Are you Ready to Succeed in Music or your Industry?

Are you ready to succeed in music or your industry, turn your creativity into money, and thrive in the industry? Whether you're a content creator, social media entrepreneur, or visionary looking to build wealth and influence.

What if there is an easy way to elevate your journey and build your brand, increase your influence, income and impact?

Now there is! Inside this book, you will learn...

- Discover how this periodical book helps emerging social media and content creators create wealth and boost their influence, income, and impact.

- Gain tools and motivation to build multiple income streams, monetize your craft, and leverage AI for wealth.

- Unlock how to build a lasting personal brand that stands out in a saturated content digital world.

- The twelve zodiac signs and a 14-day adventure, a timeless guide and reference blending strategy, heritage, and unity.

- Be inspired by top artists and leaders sharing secrets for living an extraordinary life.

- And so much more!

The book is written in a clear and easy-to-understand style with practical tips and real-life examples, and it is your ultimate companion for achieving extraordinary results. Your path to influence, income, and legacy starts here!

Grab Your Copy Now & Take the First Step Toward Wealth and Success in the AI Age!

> "Go and wake up your luck!"
> –Persian **Proverb**

Chuntianle (New Power Art)

chuntianlec@gmail.com

Spring Impression

WHAT OTHERS ARE SAYING ABOUT

Chuntianle & New Power Art STRATEGIES

"Chuntianle unites renowned and emerging voices, offering invaluable insight and inspiration—a force that fuels passion and strengthens the global creative community. Creating Wealth, a period book for emerging social media and content creators, a transformational guide for hope, future and success."

–Da'en C.

"Chuntianle's dedication to help artists in business to build wealth and brand and create an inclusive community is remarkable. The Spring Impression Event was a shining example of her commitment to weave Eastern and Western cultures. Her strategies for promoting hope and resilience through art and music have truly helped to increase income, influence and impact and made your community stronger and more united."

–Jing W.

"Chuntianle's vision of integrating Eastern and Western cultures provided a wonderful platform for artists to showcase your work. Her strategies for encouraging creativity and resilience are truly commendable."

–Thomas Marwedel

"Chuntianle (New Power Art) ideas are an essential guidance-bridging musical achievement with personal evolution."

–De Munter Alfons
Fons Plays Guitar

"Chuntianle's music I can describe as ethereal. Dreamy little waterfalls of poetry. Her several original compositions really stand out in her strong style always imbedded in nature and holistic healing, always having the strong positive flow from one heart to another. Although the compositions have a classical feel to it, her vocal performance is typical Chinese. She also takes up the challenge to sing soprano works from the great composers such as Schubert in which she really shines. So almost two different worlds but it's a good marriage in which her talent shows. call it art, call it power, call it new… call it New Power Art."

–John Schuur

Process engineer, Chemistry & Physics teacher

"Chuntianle's strategies (New Power Art） are transformative and practical— a catalyst for both professional and personal growth."

–Emin Dinlersoz

Ph.D. Economist

"Chuntianle's vision has been a game-changer. Her innovative approach to building a global community through music and art has allowed artists to succeed beyond borders and expand brands."

–Gary Rominger

Senior Program Manager

"Chuntianle's concepts (New Power Art) spark success."

–Marco Isidori

Marine Biologist

"Refreshing approaches propel music excellence and harmonize with personal growth, Chuntianle's (New Power Art) ideas are the transformational guide."

–Panagiotis_Charlavanis

Greek_Singer

"New Power Art's (Chuntianle) strategies resonate on a different level. Success in Music bridges the gap between talent and triumph. Bravo!"

–John Lemon

Deepsong Productions

"Chuntianle's (New Power Art) ingenious strategies in 'Success in Music' revolutionize the way musicians approach their craft. Her innovative ideas seamlessly intertwine music mastery with personal growth, offering a roadmap for success that transcends conventional norms. This book isn't just about music; it's a profound exploration of mindset and methodology, guiding musicians toward excellence. Chuntianle's transformative thoughts inspire aspiring artists to embrace their potential fully. A must-read for people seeking a holistic approach to musical success. " from YouTube 'fadaa Zahira'

–Q.ZAHIRA

"New Power Art's (Chuntianle) concepts are a compass for navigating success in music and personal growth."

–Kemal Demirkol

@kemaldemirkoling

"Chuntianle's (New Power Art) strategies redefine success, offering a dynamic blend of innovation and practical wisdom."

–Daniel P.

"New Power Art's (Chuntianle) strategic brilliance offers a roadmap for aspiring musicians, blending innovation with practicality for success."

–Bret Grabowski

Potential Reality YouTube channel creator

"Beautiful doesn't even begin to describe her music and compositions. Chuntianle has a mastery of music as a language that speaks to the heart."

–Elizabeth A. Gregor

Ph.D. in Chemistry

"Chuntianle's (New Power Art) thoughts change people's life"

–Michael Lucas

MOTIVATE AND INSPIRE OTHERS!
"Share This Book"

Retail $24.95

Special Order

To Place an Order Contact:
chuntianlec@gmail.com
YouTube.com/@NewPowerArt
Instagram.com/NewPowerArt

THE IDEAL PROFESSIONAL SPEAKER FOR YOUR NEXT EVENT!

Any organization that wants to develop their people to become "extraordinary," needs to hire (Chuntianle, New Power Art) for a keynote and/or workshop training!

TO CONTACT OR BOOK
(Chuntianle, New Power Art)
TO SPEAK:

(chuntianlec@gmail.com)

(YouTube.com/@NewPowerArt)

(Instagram.com/NewPowerArt)

THE IDEAL
COACH
(or Consultant)
FOR YOU!

If you're ready to overcome challenges, have major breakthroughs and achieve higher levels, then you will love having (Chuntianle, New Power Art) **as your coach!**

TO CONTACT
(Chuntianle, New Power Art)

(chuntianlec@gmail.com)

(YouTube.com/@NewPowerArt)

(Instagram.com/NewPowerArt)

11

Dedication

In the quiet dawn and starlit nights, your blend of love and wisdom touches me deeply. With immense respect and gratitude, I dedicate this book to my wonderful family.

Your unwavering support and love nurtured my dreams. Your guidance, like a steady lighthouse, steered my journey, filling my sails with a gentle breeze. Every memory and encouragement fueled this endeavor.

In my life, your presence shines the brightest. You've shown me how to be strong in tough times, kind in chaos, and the power of staying together. Without your guidance and all our shared moments of happiness, I wouldn't be here writing this book.

This dedication goes beyond words; with each sentence, I honor your legacy and carry your immeasurable love forward.

I love you. with boundless appreciation.

Chuntianle

Table of Contents

A Message to You

My Message

I love spring, I compose music, and I sing my own songs as a soprano. People often have asked me questions about music, my composition, and how to succeed in music. I hope this book makes a positive difference in your life!

Woman with a Parasol - Madame Monet and Her Son
September 2023. Original Piano Music
Spring Impression Art Festival in March 2024

"A single spark can start a prairie fire"! I strongly believe that top achievers and millionaires think and act differently, which is why they reach higher levels of success. This book offers simple yet powerful strategies to elevate your business performance. My goal is to inspire and empower you to be more, do more, and achieve more.

When I was a little girl, my family and I attended an acrobatic event. Among the incredible performances, there was one that I'll never forget.

It involved a young acrobat attempting to climb a ladder. Here's

17

the twist: there was nothing holding it up - no wall, no support. The ladder wobbled and swayed, and the acrobat faced a real challenge keeping his balance as he tried to climb. He slipped, stumbled, and fell back to the ground multiple times. The crowd had mixed reactions. Some folks cheered him on with genuine support, while others couldn't resist and applauded with sarcastic screaming. The pressure on the acrobat was undoubtedly huge, but what stood out was his unwavering determination.

As I watched him pick himself up after each fall and courageously return to the ladder, I couldn't help but feel a deep appreciation for his perseverance. I wondered if he even knew what the cause of the problem was.

What this means to you is, to succeed in music, you, just like the acrobat, need the ladder and the way to climb the ladder.

In that moment, I learned a valuable lesson about the human spirit. It wasn't just about the ladder; not only was it solely about his acrobatic skills, but also about the unyielding spirit within us, the burning desire to reach new heights, and the commitment to overcome the difficulty. That young acrobat became a symbol of persistence in my heart, a reminder that with determination and the right guidance, you can climb even the most challenging ladders.

I also remember when my parents introduced me to classical music, operas, and timeless ballads. Music has always been my

18

peaceful bay in tough times and a source of joy in happy moments. It's been my voice when words fail, my comfort when I'm alone, and my way of celebrating togetherness.

As I grew up, my love for music grew deeper. I started exploring the piano and diving into the creative process of composing, even though I wanted to have my own unique music style.

What it means to you is that music is a type of art, which is an extension of human emotions, and a way to express human emotions. You are all artists in your own way. To succeed in music, your heart needs to feel a strong connection between your emotions, the natural rhythms of the world like the four seasons, and the evolving journey of your artist life.

On a fresh spring morning, the idea for my book, "Success in Music," started to form. I sat by the window, sipping tea, watching the colorful flowers bloom as winter faded away. It hit me how the seasons changing is a lot like the ups and downs in our lives. My journey from self-discovery to creative highs combined with my love for music, led me to write my first book "Success in Music" for those who want to succeed in music.

My mission is to help you succeed in music and personal growth. I'm here to make the music world less confusing by giving you clear advice and practical tips. I want to show you how to mix your love for music with smart business insights.

In that book, I shared with you steps, 25 chapters, not only to succeed in music, but also to better your life. Step by step, this book unlocked the secrets and the strategies of the music industry. It's a compass designed to guide aspiring musicians towards success. The stories in this book tell the real experiences of those who ventured into the music industry.

My goal is to encourage you to become the greatest person you can be, to stand out from the crowd. After my first book, I wrote second and third book, "Music Festival in AI Age", "Sparkfire", They are not just books; They are messages of hope, personal growth, a roadmap for your creative development, and an invitation to join us on a journey to make the world a better, more harmonious place.

Now my new book "Creating Wealth: The Secret Code of Success in the AI Age & Timeless Wisdom", I invite you to join this journey of transformation, explore your potential, enjoy the periodical for social medial and content creators, create wealth, and let music be your guide through the seasons of life. Together, you will create a world where dreams become real, and the magic of music turns your lives into a beautiful melody. The ladder may be wobbly, and the path uncertain, but your dream is within reach. You are the acrobat, and your dream of succeeding in music is the ladder. With the right knowledge, guidance, and unwavering determination, you can climb that ladder and make your dream a reality.

Welcome to "Creating Wealth: The Secret Code of Success in The AI Age & Timeless Wisdom", a guide to change lives, a roadmap to success, and a call to build more wealth, a more harmonious world. It's a pleasure to connect with you through this book. I hope to meet you in person someday. Thank you for reading. You are welcome to share it with your friends and family to help them in their life.

The 4th Periodical Book Empowering Emerging Social Media Creators

This book is inspired by my book Success in Music Made Simple with the same mission.

You may also remember me that I organized and hosted the International Spring Impression Music & Art Festival. It is a great honor to write the book "Music Festival in AI Age: A Transformational Guide for Success in Music Beyond Borders and Build Your Brand."

On top of it, I wrote my 3rd book , Sparkfire Art, Wealth and Success. You may remember me that I organized and hosted the International 4 Season Impression Art Event, and interviewed social medial and content creators.

Now, spring is here, I organize International Spring Impression Art Event, my 4th book is coming soon. "Creating Wealth: The

Secret Code of Success in The AI Age and Timeless Wisdom", "A Periodical Book for Social Media and Content Creators: A Transformational Guide to Build Your Brand and Increase your Influence, Income, and Impact. This book provides valuable resources to social media and content creators, shares how to create wealth, unlock the secret code of success in the AI age and timeless wisdom, offers you in a service-oriented format, and creates a platform for people with dream.

On one hand, this book upholds core values; on the other hand, delivers those values with a mindset of service, learn from the masters, learn from the timeless wisdom inspired by the Year of Snake, follow the right path, stay true to your values, and communicate authentically.

In this book you might see your old and new friends, so this book is for you and it is our book too, it is the homeland for Social Media and Content Creators, The Periodical Book Empowering Emerging Social Media Creators.

Welcome to join the incredible journey!

> **"Come together, take charge of your destiny,**
> **Build your brand and shape your future."**
>
> **Chuntianle (New Power Art)**

SECRET
ONE

CREATING WEALTH

THE SECRET CODE OF SUCCESS IN THE AI AGE & TIMELESS WISDOM

A PERIODICAL FOR SOCIAL MEDIA AND CONTENT CREATORS

A TRANSFORMATIONAL GUIDE TO BUILD BRAND, AND INCREASE INCOME, INFLUENCE, AND IMPACT

Secret 1 Introduction: The Year of the Snake – A Time for Transformation

The Year of the Snake is a time of wisdom, transformation, and strategic action. In Chinese culture, the snake represents intelligence, adaptability, and patience—qualities essential for success. Unlike impulsive animals, the snake moves with precision, waiting for the right moment to act. This mindset is powerful for content creators and social media entrepreneurs who want to grow their influence, build their brand, and create long-term success.

In the fast-moving world of social media, trends come and go. However, those who approach their work with strategy and persistence will thrive. Just like the snake sheds its skin to grow, creators must be willing to adapt, refine their approach, and embrace new opportunities. The Year of the Snake reminds us that success is not about rushing ahead but about making smart, calculated moves that lead to sustainable growth.

1. What Does the Year of the Snake Symbolize?

The Snake in the Chinese zodiac is often associated with wisdom, deep thinking, and transformation. It represents the ability to navigate challenges with intelligence and grace. This symbolism is particularly relevant to social media and content creation, where persistence and strategic decision-making define success.

Unlike other zodiac animals known for impulsiveness or brute strength, the snake is calculated. It waits, observes, and acts at the right moment. Content creators can learn from this approach. Instead of chasing every trend blindly, successful creators focus on long-term vision, positioning themselves as industry leaders, and crafting content that remains valuable over time.

2. Harnessing Wisdom, Strategy, and Adaptability for Success

The most successful content creators don't just follow trends; they create them. They are strategic, patient, and focused on long-term goals. Here are three key lessons from the Year of the Snake that can help you achieve success in social media and content creation:

a. Wisdom: Build a Strong Brand

Your brand is more than just your logo or aesthetic—it's the essence of who you are and what you stand for. As a creator, your unique voice, values, and perspective set you apart. The snake's ability to shed its skin reminds us that branding isn't static; it evolves. Take time to refine your brand identity so it reflects your growth and ambitions.

Wisdom is gained through experience, learning, and observation. In the digital world, this means understanding your audience, mastering your platform, and staying informed about industry changes. Instead of jumping from one trend to another without direction, take the time to study what works.

Ask yourself:

- Who is my ideal audience?
- What type of content resonates with them?
- How can I provide value consistently?

Successful content creators are always learning. They analyze their metrics, seek feedback, and refine their message. They don't rely on luck; they build expertise and use it to make informed decisions.

b. Strategy: Plan for the Long Term

A snake never moves without purpose. Similarly, great content creators don't post randomly—they have a plan. Having a content strategy means knowing what you want to achieve and creating a roadmap to get there.

Your strategy should include:

- A clear content calendar with scheduled posts
- A consistent brand message and style
- Engagement tactics to build a loyal audience

26

- Monetization plans to turn your content into income

Many creators give up too soon because they don't see immediate results. The Year of the Snake teaches us to stay patient and persistent. Success in social media is a marathon, not a sprint.

c. Adaptability: Embrace Change and Innovation

The digital world is constantly evolving. New platforms emerge, algorithms change, and audience preferences shift. Instead of resisting change, successful creators embrace it.

Being adaptable means:

- Experimenting with new content formats (e.g., short videos, live streams, interactive posts)
- Learning new skills (e.g., video editing, SEO, marketing)
- Diversifying your platforms to reach a wider audience
- Adjusting strategies based on data and feedback

The ability to pivot and evolve is what separates those who survive from those who thrive. Stay open-minded, and don't be afraid to try new things.

3. The Power of Long-Term Vision and Action

One of the biggest mistakes content creators make is focusing only on short-term success. Viral videos and overnight fame might seem exciting, but they rarely lead to lasting impact. The most successful social media influencers and content creators understand the importance of long-term vision.

a.   Consistency is Key

Posting once in a while and expecting results won't work. Building a brand requires consistent effort over time. This means showing up regularly, delivering valuable content, and engaging with your audience.

Think of it like planting seeds. You may not see results immediately, but if you nurture your content, it will grow into something significant.

b.   Take Action Every Day

Dreaming about success is not enough. You need to take action. Set small, achievable goals and work toward them daily. Whether it's writing a blog post, filming a video, or engaging with your audience, every action counts.

Ask yourself:

• What is one thing I can do today to move closer to my goals?

- How can I improve my content this week?
- What skills do I need to learn to take my brand to the next level?

c. **Stay Resilient**

Rejections, setbacks, and slow growth are part of the journey. The Year of the Snake teaches us resilience. When faced with obstacles, don't give up—adapt, improve, and keep moving forward.

4. Join the Movement

The Year of the Snake is the perfect time to transform your creative journey. Whether you are just starting or looking to take your brand to new heights, this book will guide you through the steps to success.

Remember, success doesn't happen overnight, but with wisdom, strategy, and adaptability, you can achieve lasting wealth and impact in the world of social media and content creation. Let's make this year one of growth, opportunity, and success!

Spring is Here, Join Us at the International Spring Impression Art Festival 2025 (February, 11)

Chinese New Year, The Year of Snake January 2025

CREATING WEALTH

THE SECRET CODE OF SUCCESS IN THE AI AGE & TIMELESS WISDOM

A PERIODICAL FOR SOCIAL MEDIA AND CONTENT CREATORS

A TRANSFORMATIONAL GUIDE TO BUILD BRAND, AND INCREASE INCOME, INFLUENCE, AND IMPACT

Secret 2 How Do You Stand Out in a Saturated Content World?

Social media is more crowded than ever. Millions of creators are competing for attention, making it harder to stand out. But the Year of the Snake brings a unique opportunity. The snake is known for its wisdom, adaptability, and strategic mindset—qualities that are essential for success in the digital world.

Standing out in this competitive space requires a combination of authenticity, strategy, and consistency. People are drawn to content that feels real, unique, and valuable. If you want to attract a loyal audience, ask yourself:

- **What makes my content different?** Identify your niche and personal style.

- **How does my content provide value?** Teach, entertain, or inspire your audience.
- **Am I showing my true self?** Audiences connect with authenticity.

The snake teaches us to be patient and calculated. Instead of rushing to post random content, take time to plan and refine your message. Engagement matters more than vanity metrics like follower counts.

1. The Biggest Mistakes That Hold Creators Back

Many content creators struggle to gain traction, not because they lack talent, but because they fall into common traps. Here are some mistakes that might be holding you back:

a. Lack of Consistency

The snake moves with intention and steadiness. Similarly, success in social media requires regular posting and engagement. Inconsistent posting confuses your audience and causes them to lose interest. Choose a manageable schedule—whether it's daily, weekly, or bi-weekly—and stick to it.

b. Focusing Only on Virality

Chasing viral content can be tempting, but it's not a long-term strategy. The snake doesn't strike randomly—it moves with purpose. Instead of trying to go viral, focus on building a strong foundation. A smaller, engaged audience is more valuable than millions of uninterested followers.

c. **Neglecting Engagement**

Social media isn't just about broadcasting—it's about conversation. If you're not responding to comments, engaging with followers, or interacting with other creators, you're missing out on growth. Relationships build trust, and trust leads to a loyal audience although time is always a challenge.

2. The Content Strategies That Work in the Year of the Snake

To succeed, content creators need to think strategically, just like the snake. Here are some powerful strategies to adopt:

a. . **Build a Strong Personal Brand**

Your brand is what sets you apart from others. It's not just your logo or colors—it's your voice, values, and the way you connect with your audience. Define your brand identity and be consistent across all platforms.

b. . Tell Your Story

People connect with stories. Share your journey, struggles, and victories. The Year of the Snake reminds us that transformation is powerful. Show your audience how you've grown and evolved, and they'll be inspired to follow your journey.

c. Leverage Multiple Platforms

Relying on just one platform is risky. Algorithms change, accounts get suspended, and trends shift. Diversify your presence across different platforms—YouTube, TikTok, Instagram, LinkedIn, and even your own website or email list.

d. Create Evergreen Content

Trendy content fades quickly, but evergreen content stays relevant for years. Tutorials, how-to guides, and educational content are great long-term assets that will continue bringing in views and followers over time.

e. Use AI and Automation Wisely

AI tools can help streamline your content creation process. Use AI for video editing, writing assistance, or scheduling posts, but don't lose the human touch. The snake adapts, but it remains true to its nature. Use AI as a tool, not a replacement for authenticity.

f. Monetize Smartly

Growing an audience is great, but turning it into income is even better. There are many ways to monetize:

- **Brand collaborations** – Partner with companies that align with your values.
- **Affiliate marketing** – Earn commissions by recommending products.
- **Digital products** – Sell ebooks, courses, or exclusive content.
- **Memberships & subscriptions** – Offer premium content for paying subscribers.

3. Final Thoughts

The Year of the Snake is a time for transformation, wisdom, and strategic action. If you apply these principles, you can stand out, avoid common mistakes, and build a successful, sustainable career as a content creator. Social media success isn't about luck—it's about smart planning, adaptability, and persistence.

Now, take the first step. Define your vision, commit to your growth, and embrace the journey ahead. The road to success is waiting, and the Year of the Snake is the perfect time to seize your opportunity.

SECRET
THREE

CREATING WEALTH

THE SECRET CODE OF SUCCESS IN THE AI AGE & TIMELESS WISDOM

A PERIODICAL FOR SOCIAL MEDIA AND CONTENT CREATORS

A TRANSFORMATIONAL GUIDE TO BUILD BRAND, AND INCREASE INCOME, INFLUENCE, AND IMPACT

Secret 3 Monetization & Wealth Building for Creators

The Year of the Snake represents wisdom, strategy, and adaptability, patience—these qualities that are essential for building wealth as a content creator. Many people think success in social media is all about going viral, but the reality is that sustainable wealth comes from a well-planned monetization strategy. In this chapter, we will explore how successful creators make real money, the difference between passive and active income, and the best monetization models for social media and content creators.

1. How Do Successful Creators Make Real Money?

Many creators start their journey with a passion for making videos, writing blogs, or creating art. However, passion alone does not pay the bills. To make real money, you need a monetization strategy. The most successful content creators understand that their content is a business. They diversify their income streams, create valuable content that people are willing to pay for, and build strong relationships with their audience.

One of the key factors in making money as a creator is consistency. Posting high-quality content regularly helps build trust and engagement. Additionally, successful creators know their audience. They understand what their followers need, what problems they can solve, and how they can add value to their

38

lives. This is what turns casual viewers into loyal fans and paying customers.

Passive vs. Active Income Streams for Content Creators

There are two main types of income creators can generate: active and passive income.

- **Active Income:** This type of income requires direct effort. For example, when you do sponsored content, offer coaching services, or work on freelance projects, you are earning active income. You get paid for the work you do in real-time.
- **Passive Income:** This is money that continues to come in even when you're not actively working. Examples include ad revenue, affiliate marketing, selling digital products, and memberships. Passive income allows creators to make money while they sleep.

A smart creator balances both types of income. Active income provides immediate financial stability, while passive income ensures long-term sustainability. Over time, as passive income grows, it can provide financial freedom, allowing creators to focus on their passion without financial stress.

2. Monetization Models: Sponsorships, Digital Products, Ads, Memberships, and More

There are many ways to monetize content, and the best approach is to combine multiple income streams. Let's break down some of the most effective monetization methods:

a. Sponsorships and Brand Deals

- Brands pay creators to promote their products or services.
- Successful sponsorships require a strong, engaged audience and content that aligns with the brand.
- Even small creators can land sponsorships if they have a niche, dedicated following.

b. Digital Products

- Selling eBooks, courses, templates, or exclusive content is a great way to earn money.
- Digital products require effort upfront but can generate passive income over time.
- The key is to create something valuable that solves a problem for your audience.

c. Ad Revenue

- Platforms like YouTube, TikTok, and blogs offer ad monetization.
- The more views you get, the higher your earnings.
- While ad revenue alone is not always enough, it can be a good passive income stream.

d. **Memberships and Subscriptions**

- Platforms like Patreon, YouTube Memberships, and Buy Me a Coffee allow fans to support creators directly.
- Creators can offer exclusive content, behind-the-scenes access, and special perks.
- This model works best for creators with a loyal, engaged audience.

e. **Affiliate Marketing**

- Promoting products or services and earning a commission for every sale made through your unique link.
- Works well in niches like tech reviews, fashion, and online tools.
- The key is to recommend products you genuinely believe in.

f. **Freelance Services and Consulting**

- Creators with expertise in a field can offer consulting, coaching, or freelance services.
- This includes graphic design, video editing, writing, social media management, and more.
- This is a great way to generate active income while building a reputation.

3. How to Turn Followers into Paying Fans and Clients

One of the biggest challenges creators face is converting their audience into paying customers. Here's how you can do it:

a. Build Trust

- Be authentic and provide real value.
- Engage with your audience and create content that speaks to their needs.

b. Create a Clear Offer

- Make it easy for your audience to buy from you.
- Whether it's a course, a product, or a service, ensure your offer is clear and solves a problem.

c. Use Call-to-Actions (CTAs)

- Always tell your audience what to do next. Should they subscribe? Buy? Sign up?
- Effective CTAs guide people toward making a purchase decision.

d. **Leverage Email Marketing**

- Social media algorithms change, but email lists give you direct access to your audience.
- Send valuable content, promotions, and updates directly to your subscribers.

e. **Provide Exclusive Value**

- Offer bonuses, discounts, or early access to encourage people to become paying members.
- Make your paying audience feel special.

4. Final Thoughts

The Year of the Snake reminds us to be strategic, patient, and adaptable—qualities that are essential for financial success as a content creator. Making money online is possible for anyone willing to put in the effort, learn the right strategies, and stay consistent. By combining active and passive income streams, choosing the right monetization models, and turning followers into paying fans, you can build a sustainable and profitable career in the digital world.

In the next chapter, we'll explore how to grow and engage your audience effectively. Remember, success is not just about making money—it's about creating value and a lasting impact.

Chuntianle (New Power Art)

chuntianlec@gmail.com

CREATING WEALTH

THE SECRET CODE OF SUCCESS IN THE AI AGE & TIMELESS WISDOM

A PERIODICAL FOR SOCIAL MEDIA AND CONTENT CREATORS

A TRANSFORMATIONAL GUIDE TO BUILD BRAND, AND INCREASE INCOME, INFLUENCE, AND IMPACT

Secret 4 .The Power of Your Avatar and The Big Lies

In the digital world, your **avatar** is more than just a profile picture or a brand logo—it is the identity you craft to connect with your audience. A well-defined avatar allows you to establish credibility, attract the right followers, and build an engaged community. But many content creators and social media entrepreneurs make critical mistakes when shaping their online personas.

1. The Power of Your Avatar: Who Do You Want to Serve?

Your avatar should answer these key questions:

a. **What do you stand for?**

   What core principles or beliefs define your mission and drive your actions?

b. **What problem do you solve?**

   What specific challenge or pain point does your product, service, or message address for your avatar?

c. **What emotions do you evoke?**

   How do you make your avatar feel—hopeful, inspired, relieved, empowered, etc.?

d. **What values do you represent?**

   What ethical beliefs or values are at the heart of your brand and resonate deeply with your avatar?

46

While crafting your avatar, you must avoid falling into traps that can limit your growth. Let's uncover the **Big Lies, Big Excuses, and Big Promises** that often hold content creators back.

2. The Big Lies That Hold You Back

a. "You Have to Be an Expert Before You Start"

Many aspiring content creators believe they must achieve a certain level of mastery before they share their knowledge. The truth? You don't need to be an expert; you just need to be one step ahead of your audience. Share your journey, show your learning process, and document rather than create.

b. "The Market is Too Saturated"

While it's true that competition exists, uniqueness lies in your perspective, experience, and personality. Instead of focusing on saturation, focus on differentiation. No one else has your exact voice, story, and approach.

c. "AI Will Take Over Everything—Why Even Try?"

AI is a tool, not a replacement. Creators who learn how to use AI enhance their work, not erase their opportunities. AI can help automate repetitive tasks, generate ideas, and optimize content—

but your creativity, authenticity, and strategic thinking are irreplaceable.

3. The Big Excuses That Stop You

a. "I Don't Have Enough Time"

If something is important, you make time for it. Content creation doesn't require 10 hours a day—just consistency. Start with small, manageable commitments and build up from there.

b. "I'm Not Good on Camera or Social Media"

Everyone starts somewhere. Perfection is not required—authenticity is. If you're not comfortable on video, start with audio, blogs, or written posts. Your voice matters, no matter the medium.

c. "I Need Better Equipment First"

You don't need the best camera, lighting, or software to start. Your smartphone and creativity are enough. Upgrade as you grow, but don't let a lack of expensive tools be an excuse.

4. The Big Promises You Must Keep

a. Deliver Value Consistently

Your audience follows you because they trust you. Never break that trust. If you promise education, entertainment, or inspiration—deliver it consistently.

b. Stay True to Your Mission

Don't chase every new trend that doesn't align with your brand. Stay authentic to your purpose, and you will attract an audience that genuinely resonates with you.

c. Keep Learning and Evolving

The AI age is constantly changing. Stay adaptable, keep learning, and embrace new technologies. Success comes to those who evolve and innovate.

5. Final Thoughts

Creating wealth and impact in the AI age requires more than just talent—it demands strategy, persistence, and adaptability. By crafting a strong avatar, avoiding the big lies, learning from big mistakes, overcoming big excuses, and delivering on big promises, you will position yourself for success in content creation and beyond.

The future belongs to those who show up, stay consistent, and provide value. Will you be one of them?

Chuntianle (New Power Art)

chuntianlec@gmail.com

Spring Impression

CREATING WEALTH

THE SECRET CODE OF SUCCESS IN THE AI AGE & TIMELESS WISDOM

A PERIODICAL FOR SOCIAL MEDIA AND CONTENT CREATORS

A TRANSFORMATIONAL GUIDE TO BUILD BRAND, AND INCREASE INCOME, INFLUENCE, AND IMPACT

Secret 5 Building a Powerful Personal Brand

In today's digital world, content creation is booming. Millions of people share videos, blogs, and social media posts every day. But with so much content, how do you make sure your voice is heard? The answer is branding.

1.   Why Branding is More Important Than Ever

Your personal brand is your identity online. It's how people recognize and remember you. More than just a logo or a color scheme, your brand is the story you tell, the emotions you create, and the value you offer. A strong personal brand sets you apart from the crowd, builds trust, and turns casual viewers into loyal fans and customers.

Without a strong brand, you are just another creator in the sea of content. With a powerful brand, you become unforgettable.

2.   The 3 Key Elements of a Magnetic Personal Brand

Creating a successful personal brand isn't about being famous—it's about being known for something valuable. Here are the three essential elements to building a brand that attracts the right audience:

a.   Clarity: Know Who You Are and What You Stand For

The first step to building a strong brand is understanding who you are and what you offer. Ask yourself:

- What topics or industries am I passionate about?
- What unique perspective or skills do I bring?
- What kind of audience do I want to attract?

Your brand should reflect your personality and values. If you love creativity and innovation, showcase that in your content. If you're passionate about helping others, make that a core part of your message. The clearer you are about your identity, the easier it is for your audience to connect with you.

b. Consistency: Show Up the Same Way, Everywhere

Successful brands are recognizable. This means your tone, visuals, and message should be consistent across all platforms.

- **Visuals:** Use the same colors, fonts, and styles for your social media, website, and promotional materials.
- **Tone of Voice:** Whether you are informative, funny, inspirational, or professional, your tone should be the same in all your content.
- **Content Theme:** Stick to your niche. If you're a tech reviewer, don't suddenly switch to cooking tutorials. Consistency builds trust and helps people know what to expect from you.

c. Connection: Build Relationships with Your Audience

Branding is more than just looking good—it's about creating relationships. Your audience wants to feel connected to you. Engage with them by:

- Responding to comments and messages.
- Sharing personal stories and experiences.
- Creating content that solves their problems or inspires them.
- Encouraging interaction through questions, polls, and community discussions.

When people feel a connection with you, they are more likely to support you, share your work, and buy from you.

3. How to Create a Brand That's Memorable and Profitable

Having a strong personal brand isn't just about looking professional—it also helps you make money. Here's how to ensure your brand is not only memorable but also financially successful:

a. Define Your Niche and Target Audience

Find a specific niche that aligns with your skills and interests. The more focused your niche, the easier it is to attract the right audience. Instead of just saying "I make lifestyle content," try "I help busy professionals simplify their lives with productivity tips."

A clear niche makes it easier for brands and followers to understand what you do and why they should follow you.

b. Create High-Value Content

Your brand is built through content. The more valuable your content, the more people will trust and support you. Focus on creating, such as:

- Informative videos or blog posts.
- Entertaining and engaging content.
- Inspirational or motivational content that resonates with people.

The better your content, the stronger your brand will be.

c. Leverage Social Proof and Testimonials

People trust brands that others trust. Showcasing testimonials, collaborations, and reviews builds credibility. If a brand or influencer has worked with you, highlight it. If followers have had success using your tips or products, share their stories.

d. Monetize Your Brand

Once your brand is established, start monetizing it. Some ways include:

- Offering digital products like e-books or courses.
- Getting sponsorships and brand deals.
- Selling merchandise.
- Providing consulting or coaching services.

A strong brand makes it easier to earn money because people trust you and see you as an authority.

4.   Final Thoughts

Building a powerful personal brand takes time, but the rewards are worth it. In the Year of the Snake, embrace strategy, adaptability, and wisdom to create a brand that stands out. Be clear about who you are, stay consistent, and build meaningful connections. Your brand is your key to success—make it strong, make it memorable, and watch it open doors to new opportunities.

CREATING WEALTH

THE SECRET CODE OF SUCCESS IN THE AI AGE & TIMELESS WISDOM

A PERIODICAL FOR SOCIAL MEDIA AND CONTENT CREATORS

A TRANSFORMATIONAL GUIDE TO BUILD BRAND, AND INCREASE INCOME, INFLUENCE, AND IMPACT

Secret 6 AI & The Future of Content Creation

The rise of artificial intelligence (AI) has changed the way we create, share, and market content. In the Year of the Snake, which represents wisdom, transformation, and strategy, embracing AI can be a game-changer for content creators. But how do we use it effectively? Will AI replace human creativity? And how can we maintain authenticity in an era of automation? Let's explore how AI is shaping the future of content creation and how you can stay ahead.

1. How AI Is Changing Content Creation and Marketing

AI is no longer a futuristic concept—it's already here, and it's everywhere. From video editing tools to AI-generated blog posts, technology is making content creation faster, smarter, and more efficient. Here's how AI is transforming the industry:

- **Automated Content Creation:** AI can now generate blog posts, scripts, and even music in seconds. Tools like ChatGPT and Jasper AI help creators brainstorm ideas, draft content, and optimize writing for engagement.
- **Video & Image Editing:** AI-powered apps like Canva, Runway, and Adobe Sensei can edit photos and videos, remove backgrounds, and even generate animations—all with just a few clicks.

- **Personalized Marketing:** AI analyzes audience behavior to create highly targeted ads and recommendations. Platforms like YouTube, TikTok, and Instagram use AI algorithms to push content to the right viewers at the right time.

- **SEO & Analytics:** AI tools like Surfer SEO and Google's RankBrain help creators optimize their content for search engines, making it easier to reach more people. AI-driven analytics tools provide deep insights into audience behavior, helping creators refine their strategies.

AI is making content creation more accessible than ever, but it's not a replacement for human creativity—it's a tool that enhances it.

2. .The Current AI Tools to Save Time & Increase Engagement

If you're a content creator, you're likely juggling multiple tasks: writing, designing, editing, marketing, and engaging with your audience. AI can help you work smarter, not harder. Here are some of the best AI tools to boost your productivity:

- **Writing & Blogging:** ChatGPT, Jasper AI, Copy.ai (Generate ideas, draft content, and improve writing)
- **Video Editing:** Descript, Runway, Pictory (Automate video edits, captions, and effects)

- **Graphic Design:** Canva, Adobe Firefly (Create stunning visuals in minutes)
- **Social Media Management:** Hootsuite, Buffer (Automate posting and scheduling)
- **SEO & Marketing:** Surfer SEO, TubeBuddy, AnswerThePublic (Optimize content for search engines)
- **Voice & Music AI:** ElevenLabs, Soundraw (Generate voiceovers and AI music)

These tools allow creators to save time, improve quality, and focus on what really matters—building your brand and engaging with their audience.

3. Will AI Replace Human Creators? Staying Relevant in the AI Era

One of the biggest fears about AI is that it will replace human creators. But the truth is, AI lacks what makes content truly special—emotion, personality, and storytelling.

- **AI Can Assist, But Not Replace:** AI can generate content, but it cannot replicate human experiences, emotions, and unique perspectives. A song written by AI may sound technically correct, but it won't carry the same depth of feeling as one composed by a human.

- **Authenticity Matters More Than Ever:** In a world where AI-generated content is everywhere, audiences crave real, human stories. Creators who share their personal journeys, opinions, and emotions will stand out.

- **AI Is a Tool, Not a Threat:** Instead of fearing AI, creators should embrace it as a way to improve efficiency. AI can handle repetitive tasks, allowing creators to focus on storytelling, innovation, and building their community.

The key to staying relevant is to blend AI-powered efficiency with human creativity.

4. Ethical Concerns: Balancing Automation with Authenticity

While AI offers incredible benefits, it also raises ethical concerns. As creators, it's important to use AI responsibly and maintain transparency with your audience.

- **Misinformation:** AI-generated content can sometimes spread false information. Always fact-check and edit AI-generated materials.

- **Plagiarism & Copyright Issues:** AI pulls from existing content to generate new material. Creators must ensure they're not unintentionally copying someone else's work.

- **Over-Reliance on AI:** While AI can enhance content, relying too much on automation can make content feel robotic and impersonal.

The best approach is to use AI as a supportive tool while keeping your voice and creativity at the center of your work.

5. Final Thoughts: The Future Belongs to Smart Creators

AI is here to stay, and it will continue to evolve. The most successful content creators in the Year of the Snake will be those who embrace AI wisely—using it to enhance efficiency while maintaining authenticity.

By leveraging AI tools, staying true to your unique voice, and focusing on long-term strategy, you can navigate the changing digital landscape with confidence. The future isn't about AI replacing creators—it's about creators using AI to reach new heights.

The Year of the Snake is a time for wisdom, transformation, and adaptation. Are you ready to evolve and thrive in the AI era?

SECRET
SEVEN

CREATING WEALTH

THE SECRET CODE OF SUCCESS IN THE AI AGE & TIMELESS WISDOM

A PERIODICAL FOR SOCIAL MEDIA AND CONTENT CREATORS

A TRANSFORMATIONAL GUIDE TO BUILD BRAND, AND INCREASE INCOME, INFLUENCE, AND IMPACT

Secret 7 Growth Strategies for Social Media & Content Creators

Growing on social media isn't just about getting more followers—it's about building a real community. In the Year of the Snake, which symbolizes wisdom, patience, and strategy, success comes from smart, intentional actions.

If you want to stand out in today's crowded digital space, you need a strong growth strategy. You need to understand how to attract the right audience, increase engagement, and build long-term loyalty. In this chapter, we'll break down the most effective ways to grow your social media presence and turn casual viewers into dedicated fans.

1. How to Grow Your Followers, Subscribers, and Influence

Building an audience isn't about luck—it's about strategy. Here's what you need to focus on:

- **Know Your Niche:** The best creators have a clear focus. What's your expertise? What do you want to be known for? Pick a niche that aligns with your passion and skills.
- **Post Consistently:** Social media platforms reward consistency. Whether you post daily, weekly, or somewhere in between, stick to a schedule so your audience knows when to expect new content.

- **Engage with Your Audience:** Growth isn't just about creating content—it's about interacting. Reply to comments, ask questions, and start conversations. The more engagement your content gets, the more platforms will push it to a wider audience.

- **Leverage Trends:** Stay updated with trending topics, challenges, and hashtags. But don't just copy trends—add your unique perspective to make them stand out.

- **Optimize Your Profile:** Your bio, profile picture, and banner should clearly communicate who you are and what your content is about. A strong, professional-looking profile can encourage more people to follow you.

- **Collaborate with Other Creators:** Partnering with other influencers in your niche can introduce you to new audiences. Whether it's a joint video, podcast, or shout-out, collaborations can accelerate your growth.

2. The Secrets to Going Viral and Increasing Engagement

Going viral isn't just about luck—there are proven strategies that increase your chances of reaching a massive audience.

- **Start with a Strong Hook:** The first few seconds of your video or post matter the most. Capture attention quickly with an intriguing question, bold statement, or surprising fact.

- **Tap into Emotions:** Content that makes people laugh, feel inspired, or sparks curiosity is more likely to be shared. Emotional connections drive engagement.

- **Make Your Content Shareable:** People love to share content that is funny, informative, or relatable. Keep your videos, captions, and graphics in a format that is easy to repost and tag friends in.

- **Encourage Interaction:** Ask questions, start polls, and use call-to-action statements like "Comment below" or "Tag a friend." The more engagement your content gets, the higher it will rank in the algorithm.

- **Test Different Formats:** Experiment with different types of content—short-form videos, carousels, infographics, live streams, and interactive posts. See what your audience responds to best.

- **Post at Peak Times:** Every platform has peak hours when users are most active. Research the best posting times for your audience and schedule your content accordingly.

3. **How to Turn Casual Viewers into Loyal Fans**

Having a big following is great, but real success comes from having an engaged audience. Here's how you can turn casual viewers into long-term supporters:

66

- **Be Authentic:** People connect with real, relatable creators. Don't try to be someone you're not—share your journey, struggles, and behind-the-scenes moments.

- **Build a Community:** Create a sense of belonging by interacting with your followers. Consider starting a private group, Discord channel, or email list where your biggest fans can connect with you.

- **Deliver Value:** Whether it's entertainment, education, or motivation, your content should always provide something valuable. The more you give, the more people will trust and support you.

- **Show Up Consistently:** If people see you often, they'll feel more connected to you. Whether it's through daily Instagram stories, weekly YouTube videos, or regular tweets, consistency builds loyalty.

- **Give Exclusive Content:** Reward your most engaged followers with bonus content, sneak peeks, or early access to new projects. This makes them feel special and appreciated.

- **Encourage User-Generated Content:** Ask your audience to create content related to your brand— whether it's fan art, testimonials, or duets. Featuring their content makes them feel valued and strengthens the community.

4. The Art of Storytelling and Why It's Crucial for Content Success

Storytelling is one of the most powerful tools you can use as a creator. People remember stories more than facts, and a well-told story can make your content unforgettable.

- **Make It Personal:** Share your journey—how you started, the challenges you faced, and the lessons you've learned. People love origin stories.

- **Create a Hero's Journey:** Position your audience as the hero. Show them how they can overcome struggles, reach their goals, or improve their lives through your content.

- **Use Visual Storytelling:** Whether through video, images, or graphics, make your content visually engaging. A great story paired with compelling visuals is a winning combination.

- **Keep It Simple:** The best stories are easy to follow. Don't overcomplicate things—deliver your message in a clear and relatable way.

- **End with a Strong Call-to-Action:** Every great story has a purpose. Whether it's inspiring action, driving sales, or spreading awareness, make sure your audience knows what to do next.

5. Final Thoughts

Success on social media isn't about chasing numbers—it's about building real influence. By focusing on audience engagement, creating shareable content, and mastering the art of storytelling, you can achieve long-term growth.

Remember, the Year of the Snake is all about wisdom, patience, and adaptability. Take a strategic approach to your social media growth, and your influence will expand beyond what you ever imagined.

The journey to success starts now—take action and start growing!

Chuntianle (New Power Art)

chuntianlec@gmail.com

SECRET
EIGHT

CREATING WEALTH

THE SECRET CODE OF SUCCESS IN THE AI AGE & TIMELESS WISDOM

A PERIODICAL FOR SOCIAL MEDIA AND CONTENT CREATORS

A TRANSFORMATIONAL GUIDE TO BUILD BRAND, AND INCREASE INCOME, INFLUENCE, AND IMPACT

Secret 8 Overcoming Challenges & Staying Motivated

Success in the world of social media and content creation isn't always smooth. There will be times when you feel stuck, exhausted, or even discouraged. The Year of the Snake teaches us patience, resilience, and adaptability—qualities that are essential when facing challenges.

No matter where you are in your journey, obstacles will appear. Maybe you feel burned out from constantly creating. Maybe negative comments make you question your work. Or maybe you struggle to stay consistent without feeling overwhelmed.

In this chapter, we'll talk about how to overcome these challenges so you can stay motivated and keep growing.

1. How to Deal with Burnout and Creative Blocks

Burnout is real, and it happens when you push yourself too hard without rest. Creative blocks can also be frustrating, making it hard to come up with new ideas. Here's how to manage both:

a. Signs of Burnout

- Feeling exhausted even after a full night's sleep.
- Losing excitement for creating content.
- Struggling to come up with fresh ideas.
- Feeling frustrated or overwhelmed by small tasks.

72

b. **How to Overcome Creative Blocks**

- **Step Away from the Screen:** Sometimes, the best thing you can do is take a break. Go outside, exercise, read a book—do anything that isn't related to content creation. Inspiration often comes when you're not forcing it.

- **Change Your Environment:** A new workspace or a different setting can spark creativity. Try working from a café, park, or a new room in your house.

- **Look for Inspiration Everywhere:** Watch movies, listen to music, read stories, or explore different cultures. Great ideas often come from unexpected places.

- **Brainstorm Without Pressure:** Set a timer for 10 minutes and write down as many content ideas as possible. No judgment, no overthinking—just free-flow brainstorming.

- **Collaborate with Others:** Sometimes, talking to other creators can help you break out of a creative slump. Join communities, attend events, or simply reach out to a friend for fresh perspectives.

c. **How to Prevent Burnout**

- **Set Boundaries:** Avoid working 24/7. Have a set time when you stop checking emails and social media.

- **Take Breaks:** Even small breaks throughout the day help refresh your mind. The Pomodoro technique (working for

73

25 minutes, then taking a 5-minute break) can be very effective.

- **Schedule Time Off:** Plan days where you completely unplug from social media and content creation. You'll come back feeling more energized.

- **Remember Your Why:** Reconnect with the reason you started. What impact do you want to make? Reminding yourself of your mission can reignite your passion.

2. Handling Negative Comments, Trolls, and Online Pressure

No matter how positive your content is, at some point, you'll face negativity. The internet can be a harsh place, and learning how to handle criticism is an important skill.

Types of Negative Comments & How to Respond

- **Constructive Criticism** – If someone gives feedback in a respectful way, consider it! You can learn and grow from it. Respond with appreciation or use it as an opportunity to improve.

- **Haters & Trolls** – Some people just want to provoke a reaction. The best strategy? **Ignore, block, or delete.** Don't waste your energy arguing.

- **Personal Attacks** – If someone is attacking you personally, don't engage. Instead, focus on the supportive people in your community.

- **Misinformation & Misunderstandings** – If someone spreads false information about you, calmly clarify the facts. Keep it professional and don't get defensive.

3. How to Protect Your Mental Health Online

- **Don't Take It Personally:** Negative comments often say more about the person writing them than about you.

- **Use the Mute & Block Buttons:** You don't have to entertain negativity. Protect your space.

- **Focus on Your Supporters:** For every negative person, there are likely hundreds who love your content. Don't let one bad comment outweigh all the good ones.

- **Talk to Someone You Trust:** If online negativity is affecting your mood, share your feelings with a friend or mentor.

4. How to Stay Consistent Without Feeling Overwhelmed

Consistency is key to growth, but it's important to find a balance that works for you. Here's how to stay consistent without feeling stressed:

a. **Plan Ahead**

- **Batch Create Content:** Instead of making content daily, try creating multiple pieces at once. This saves time and reduces stress.
- **Use Scheduling Tools:** Apps like Buffer, Later, or Meta's Creator Studio allow you to schedule posts in advance so you don't have to post manually every day.
- **Have a Content Calendar:** Planning what you'll post each week helps keep you organized and prevents last-minute scrambling.

b. **Work Smarter, Not Harder**

- **Repurpose Content:** Turn one idea into multiple pieces of content. A YouTube video can become a blog post, a series of Instagram stories, and a tweet.
- **Use AI Tools to Save Time:** AI can help with tasks like editing, caption writing, and idea generation. This lets you focus on creativity while automating repetitive work.
- **Create a Posting Routine:** Find a schedule that works for you—whether it's posting 3 times a week or once a day. What matters most is **consistency over time.**

c. **Stay Inspired & Motivated**

- **Surround Yourself with Positive Energy:** Follow creators who inspire you and avoid accounts that drain your energy.

- **Celebrate Small Wins:** Whether it's hitting 1,000 followers or getting your first brand deal, acknowledge your progress. Every step counts!
- **Keep Learning:** Read books, take courses, or watch tutorials to keep your skills sharp and your ideas fresh.
- **Stay Flexible:** If you need to adjust your schedule, that's okay. Growth is a marathon, not a sprint.

5. Final Thoughts

Challenges are part of every creator's journey, but how you handle them determines your success. Burnout, negativity, and inconsistency can slow you down, but with the right strategies, you can push through and keep growing.

The Year of the Snake is about wisdom and resilience. Use these principles to overcome obstacles, protect your energy, and keep creating content that inspires and connects.

Keep moving forward—your best work is still ahead of you!

Chuntianle (New Power Art)

chuntianlec@gmail.com

Spring Impression

CREATING WEALTH

THE SECRET CODE OF SUCCESS IN THE AI AGE & TIMELESS WISDOM

A PERIODICAL FOR SOCIAL MEDIA
AND CONTENT CREATORS

A TRANSFORMATIONAL GUIDE TO BUILD BRAND, AND INCREASE INCOME, INFLUENCE, AND IMPACT

Secret 9 The Year of the Snake & Your Personal Growth

The Snake is a symbol of wisdom, transformation, and resilience. In Chinese culture, those born in the Year of the Snake are known for their intelligence, adaptability, and ability to achieve success through strategic thinking. These qualities are essential for social media and content creators who want to grow, thrive, and build long-term wealth in the digital space.

Success isn't just about algorithms, engagement rates, or follower counts—it's about personal growth. The most successful content creators and entrepreneurs didn't get to where they are by luck. They embraced change, learned from failures, and constantly evolved.

In this chapter, we'll explore how you can adopt the **Snake's mindset** to transform your content, career, and life.

1.   **How to Embrace Transformation Like the Snake**

One of the most fascinating things about snakes is that they shed their skin. This is a powerful metaphor for personal growth—you must let go of old habits, fears, and limiting beliefs to step into a better version of yourself.

a.   **Signs You Need to "Shed Your Old Skin"**

- You feel stuck or uninspired in your content creation.

80

- You keep doing the same thing but aren't seeing growth.
- You fear change or stepping outside your comfort zone.
- You compare yourself too much to others and doubt your own path.

b.   **How to Transform & Grow**

- **Adopt a Learner's Mindset** – Always be open to new skills, strategies, and trends. The digital world moves fast, and those who resist change get left behind.
- **Experiment & Innovate** – Try new content formats, storytelling techniques, or platforms. Be willing to fail and learn.
- **Eliminate What's Holding You Back** – Whether it's fear of judgment, self-doubt, or procrastination, identify and work on your personal obstacles.
- **Surround Yourself with Growth-Minded People** – Join communities, collaborate with ambitious creators, and engage with those who challenge you to be better.

The Snake doesn't fear change—it thrives in it. Embrace transformation, and your success will follow.

2.   **Lessons from Successful Content Creators & Entrepreneurs**

Every successful creator has a story. They all faced struggles, failures, and moments of doubt. But what set them apart? They kept going.

Here are some powerful lessons from those who have made it:

a. They Stay Consistent Even When No One's Watching

Most content creators don't blow up overnight. Many spend years creating before they find success. The key is persistence. *Example:* Some of the biggest YouTubers started by making videos for just a handful of viewers. If they had quit early, they wouldn't be where they are today.

b. They Focus on Their Strengths

Successful creators lean into what makes them unique. Instead of copying trends blindly, they find ways to make them their own. *Lesson:* Find your unique voice, perspective, or storytelling style. That's what will make people follow you.

c. They Adapt to Change

Social media is always evolving. Platforms change their algorithms, trends come and go, and audience preferences shift. The best creators adapt instead of complaining.

Lesson: Don't get stuck in "the old way" of doing things. Keep evolving.

d. They Use Failure as Fuel

Failure isn't the opposite of success—it's part of it. Every mistake is a learning experience. *Lesson:* Instead of fearing failure, analyze what went wrong and improve. The only real failure is quitting.

e. They Build Genuine Connections

The best creators don't just chase numbers—they build communities. They make their audience feel seen, heard, and valued.
Lesson: Engage with your followers, reply to comments, and create content that serves your audience, not just yourself.

3. Mindset Shifts That Lead to Long-Term Success

Success isn't just about external actions—it starts with your mindset.

Here are some mindset shifts that will help you level up your content and career:

a. From "Quick Wins" to "Long-Term Vision"

- Many people chase viral moments, but real success comes from consistent effort over time.
- Ask yourself: *Where do I want to be in 5 years?* Start building toward that now.

b. From "Fear of Failure" to "Learning from Mistakes"

- Every creator makes mistakes. What matters is how you respond.
- Instead of saying, *"I failed,"* ask, *"What can I learn from this?"*

c. From "Comparison" to "Inspiration"

- Instead of feeling bad when you see someone else's success, study what they did right.
- Use their journey as motivation, not as a reason to doubt yourself.

d. From "Working Hard" to "Working Smart"

- Growth isn't just about working harder—it's about working smarter.
- Use tools, automation, and strategies that maximize your efficiency.

e. From "I Need to Please Everyone" to "I Need to Serve My Audience"

- Not everyone will like your content, and that's okay.
- Focus on those who love and appreciate what you do.

4. Final Thoughts

The Year of the Snake is about transformation, wisdom, and strategy. If you embrace growth, adaptability, and resilience, success will follow.

Your journey as a content creator isn't just about numbers—it's about becoming the best version of yourself. The more you evolve, learn, and push past your limits, the more success and wealth you'll attract.

So, take risks, keep creating, and remember—you are just one breakthrough away from your next big success.

Chuntianle (New Power Art)

chuntianlec@gmail.com

Spring
Impression

SECRET
TEN

CREATING WEALTH

THE SECRET CODE OF SUCCESS IN THE AI AGE & TIMELESS WISDOM

A PERIODICAL FOR SOCIAL MEDIA
AND CONTENT CREATORS

A TRANSFORMATIONAL GUIDE TO BUILD BRAND,
AND INCREASE INCOME, INFLUENCE, AND IMPACT

Chapter 10: Your Success Plan – Take Action Now!

Success in social media and content creation doesn't happen by accident. It's not just about luck or talent—it's about having a clear plan and taking consistent action.

Many people dream of becoming successful influencers, YouTubers, or digital entrepreneurs, but only a few actually achieve it. Why? Because they don't have a solid plan, or they hesitate to take action.

In this chapter, we'll create a step-by-step success plan that will help you:

- Set clear goals for content creation and monetization.
- Build influence and wealth in a structured way.
- Move from dreaming to doing—because action is everything!

1. **Set SMART Goals for Success**

Without goals, you're just posting content without direction. Successful creators have a clear vision for where they're going.

The best way to set goals is by using the SMART method:

☐ **S**pecific – Be clear about what you want.

☐ **M**easurable – Track your progress.

☐ **A**chievable – Make sure it's realistic.

☐ **R**elevant – Align your goals with your long-term vision.

☐ **T**ime-bound – Set a deadline to keep yourself accountable.

▣ Examples of SMART Goals for Creators

☐ *Vague Goal:* "I want more followers."

☐ *SMART Goal:* "I will gain 5,000 new followers on Instagram in 6 months by posting engaging reels 5 times a week and collaborating with influencers."

☐ *Vague Goal:* "I want to make money from YouTube."

☐ *SMART Goal:* "I will reach 1,000 subscribers and 4,000 watch hours in 4 months by posting high-quality videos twice a week and optimizing them for SEO."

Write down **3 SMART goals** that will take you closer to success. Keep them somewhere visible and check your progress every week!

2. **Build Influence & Wealth – A Step-by-Step Plan**

Once you have clear goals, it's time to create a step-by-step strategy to achieve them.

Step 1: Identify Your Niche & Audience

Don't try to appeal to *everyone.* Focus on a specific niche and know your audience.

- Who are they? (Age, interests, problems they need solutions for)
- What type of content do they love?
- How can you provide value and stand out?

Step 2: Create Consistently & Show Up Daily

Posting once in a while won't grow your brand**.** Success comes from consistency.

- Pick a posting schedule that works for you (daily, 3x a week, weekly).
- Engage with your audience daily (reply to comments, interact with followers).
- Batch-create content in advance so you don't get overwhelmed.

Step 3: Use the Right Growth Strategies

To grow fast, use proven content marketing tactics:

☐ Create **high-value content** that educates, entertains, or inspires.

☐ Optimize your content for **SEO** (use the right keywords, hashtags, and titles).

☐ **Leverage trends** and viral challenges to boost visibility.

☐ **Collaborate** with others to tap into new audiences.

☐ Use **hooks and storytelling** to keep people engaged.

Step 4: Monetize & Build Multiple Income Streams

Success isn't just about numbers—it's about turning your influence into income.

Here are **5 ways** to monetize your content:

☐ **Brand Deals & Sponsorships** – Partner with companies that align with your brand.

☐ **Affiliate Marketing** – Promote products and earn commissions.

☐ **Sell Your Own Products** – Courses, eBooks, merch, or coaching.

☐ **Ad Revenue** – Monetize YouTube videos, blogs, or TikTok.

☐ **Crowdfunding & Memberships** – Platforms like Patreon let fans support you directly.

Don't rely on just one income source. The most successful creators have multiple streams of income!

Step 5: Take Action – Stop Waiting & Start Doing!

Many people get stuck in planning mode. They think, research, and dream about success but never take action. The truth is:

☐ **The faster you start, the faster you improve.**

☐ **Your first videos, posts, or blogs won't be perfect, and that's okay.**

☐ **You learn by doing—not by waiting.**

3. ACTION PLAN: Start Today!

☐ **Write down your 3 SMART goals.**

☐ **Create your first (or next) piece of content today.**

☐ **Post it—even if it's not perfect.**

☐ **Engage with your audience.**

☐ **Repeat daily!**

4. Final Thoughts

You Are in Control of Your Success

Your success on social media and content creation depends on one thing: YOU.

It's not about waiting for the perfect moment or hoping for luck—it's about taking action, being consistent, and constantly improving.

The Year of the Snake is all about wisdom, strategy, and transformation. If you commit to growing, learning, and taking action, you WILL achieve the success and wealth you desire.

So, start now. Your future self will thank you!

CREATING WEALTH

THE SECRET CODE OF SUCCESS IN THE AI AGE & TIMELESS WISDOM

A PERIODICAL FOR SOCIAL MEDIA
AND CONTENT CREATORS

A TRANSFORMATIONAL GUIDE TO BUILD BRAND, AND INCREASE INCOME, INFLUENCE, AND IMPACT

Chapter 11: Your Year to Shine

The Year of the Snake is a time of wisdom, strategy, and transformation. It's about shedding the old and stepping into new opportunities—a perfect metaphor for your journey as a content creator.

If you've made it this far, you already have the passion and ambition to succeed. But reading about success isn't enough—you have to take action.

The world is waiting for your message. Your audience is out there, whether you have one follower or one million. Now is your time to shine.

In this final chapter, we'll talk about:

- Why the world needs your creativity.
- The mindset for long-term success.
- How to be part of a movement that's shaping the future.

1. **The World Needs Your Creativity**

How many times have you hesitated to post content because you thought:

- *"What if no one cares?"*
- *"What if I'm not good enough?"*

94

- *"What if I fail?"*

These doubts stop more creators than anything else. But the truth is, there is someone out there who needs your message.

Think about your favorite creators. What if they had let fear stop them? Your content has the power to inspire, educate, and entertain—but only if you share it.

Remember:

- Your story and perspective are unique.
- The right audience will connect with your content.
- Success doesn't happen overnight—it happens with consistency.

The biggest mistake is waiting for the perfect time. There is no perfect time. The perfect time is now.

2. Keep Growing, Keep Evolving

Success isn't about reaching one milestone and stopping. It's about continuous growth and reinvention.

Look at the biggest content creators today. They didn't stay the same—they evolved, adapted, and **embraced change.**

How to Keep Growing as a Creator

- **Stay curious.** Keep learning, whether it's new content strategies, AI tools, or storytelling techniques.
- **Experiment.** Test different content styles, platforms, and formats to see what works best.
- **Engage with your audience.** Listen to feedback, reply to comments, and build real relationships.
- **Take breaks when needed.** Avoid burnout by resting and finding inspiration outside of work.

Your journey doesn't end when you reach one goal—it's just the beginning of something bigger.

3. **Join the Movement – Be Part of the Future**

The world of content creation is constantly evolving, and **you have the opportunity to be at the forefront of it.**

You are not alone in this journey. There is a global community of creators, entrepreneurs, and visionaries who are building success and wealth online.

- **What Does It Mean to Be Part of This Movement?**

a. **You create content that impacts and inspires others.**
b. **You embrace new tools, trends, and opportunities.**
c. **You commit to growth, resilience, and long-term success.**

The Year of the Snake is about **strategy, wisdom, and transformation.** You already have the tools—now it's time to take action and build your future.

- **Your Next Steps**

Now that you've read this book, what will you do next?

a. **Set clear goals.** What do you want to achieve in the next 6–12 months? Write it down.
b. **Take action every day.** Even small steps—posting content, engaging with followers, or learning new skills—bring you closer to success.
c. **Surround yourself with the right people.** Join communities, network with creators, and stay inspired.

The most important step? **Just start.**

Your audience is waiting. **Your time is now.** Shine bright and make your mark in the Year of the Snake.

4. Join Me & Let's Grow Together!

I believe in the power of creativity and community. If you're ready to take your content creation journey to the next level, I invite you to join me:

- **Subscribe to my YouTube channel** – New Power Art for inspiration, music, and creator tips.

  https://www.youtube.com/@NewPowerArt

- **Follow my latest book releases & content** – Check out my books on Amazon.

  Success in Music Made Simple

  Kindle: https://www.amazon.com/dp/B0CS9ZPNF8

  Paperback: https://www.amazon.com/dp/B0CT5KVXC4

  Music Festival in AI Age

  Kindle: https://www.amazon.com/dp/B0D8VZWQYM

  Paperback: https://www.amazon.com/dp/B0D9B9ZX1C

  Sparkfire - Art, Wealth and Success

  Kindle: https: https://www.amazon.com/dp/B0DPTB4K1M

  Paperback: https://www.amazon.com/dp/B0DQJ9ZM32

- **Join the conversation** – Be part of our creative community on Facebook:

  a. Welcome to Join the Public Group: **New Power Art - Music Festival in AI Age**

  https://chuntianle-new-power-art.ck.page/ef8cb94b9f

  b. Welcome to Join the Private Group: **New Power Art - Success in Music Made Simple**

  https://chuntianle-new-power-art.ck.page/c32f586fa8

- **Stay connected** – Follow me on social media for more insights and updates.

Let's create, grow, and succeed—together!

CREATING WEALTH

THE SECRET CODE OF SUCCESS IN THE AI AGE & TIMELESS WISDOM

A PERIODICAL FOR SOCIAL MEDIA AND CONTENT CREATORS

A TRANSFORMATIONAL GUIDE TO BUILD BRAND, AND INCREASE INCOME, INFLUENCE, AND IMPACT

Secret 12 Topic: A Father's Wisdom – Lessons for Success & Wealth

A Letter from Dad to His Daughter

My daughter, listen. Life isn't just about chasing success—it's about understanding how success works and making it last. You can go fast alone, but if you want to go far, you need wisdom.

I've seen the world change. I've seen people rise and fall. And through it all, I've learned that the ones who succeed aren't always the smartest, the richest, or the luckiest—they're the ones who understand timing, patience, and the power of persistence.

So, if you want to build something meaningful—whether it's your career, your wealth, or your influence—remember these lessons. They've helped me, and they'll help you too.

1. Good Things Take Time—Don't Rush

You live in a world where everything moves fast. People want overnight success, instant fame, quick money. But that's not how the real world works.

Look at the snake—it moves slowly, but every step is precise.

Success is the same way. If you plant a seed today, don't expect a tree tomorrow. Water it, care for it, and give it time to grow.

My advice: Keep showing up. Keep improving. Success will come—but only if you're patient enough to wait for it.

2. Work Smart, Not Just Hard

When I was young, people told me, *"Work hard, and you'll succeed."* But I learned **that** hard work alone isn't enough—you have to work smart.

Imagine two fishermen:

- One wakes up early, fishes all day, but catches only a few.
- The other spends time studying where the fish gather, uses the right bait, and catches more with less effort.

102

Which one do you want to be?

My advice: Don't just work—think smart. Learn from those who have succeeded before you. Use the right tools, the right strategies, and always look for a better way.

3. Don't Just Attract Followers—Earn Their Trust

A lot of people focus on numbers—followers, views, likes. But I'll tell you something: Numbers don't mean anything if people don't trust you.

"It's better to have 100 real friends than 10,000 strangers."

A real audience isn't just people watching—it's people who believe in you. Give them value, respect them, and they'll stay with you for life.

My advice: Stop worrying about chasing followers. Instead, focus on building a community of people who actually care about your message.

4. The World Changes—You Must Change Too

One of the biggest mistakes people make? They refuse to change.

"I've always done it this way" is the most dangerous mindset you can have.

Look around. The world is moving fast. If you don't learn, if you don't adapt, you'll be left behind.

My advice: Keep your eyes open. Stay curious. The most successful people are the ones who keep learning, no matter how old or experienced they are.

5. Money Follows Value, Not the Other Way Around

So many people ask, *"How can I make more money?"* But they're asking the wrong question.

"If you chase money, it will run. But if you create value, money will follow."

Think about it—why do people pay for something? Because it helps them, entertains them, or makes their life better.

My advice: Focus on giving something valuable. Teach people something. Inspire them. Solve their problems. Do that, and wealth will come naturally.

6. Stay Calm in Tough Times

Not every day will be easy. You'll face failures, criticism, setbacks. But when trouble comes, don't panic.

The snake doesn't waste energy fighting—it waits, it watches, and it strikes at the right moment.

The same goes for you. Keep a clear head, stay patient, and make smart decisions.

My advice: When things go wrong, don't react emotionally. Step back, think, and find the best way forward.

7. True Success Is More Than Just Money

Yes, we all want financial success. But let me tell you something: Money alone won't make you happy.

True success is when you wake up excited and go to bed at peace.

If you build wealth but lose your health, your relationships, or your happiness, was it worth it?

My advice: Build a life that makes you happy—not just a bank account that looks impressive.

Final Words from Father

My child, I've shared my wisdom with you because I want you to succeed—not just in business, but in life.

So remember this:

- **Be patient.** Good things take time.
- **Work smart.** Find the best way, not just the hardest way.
- **Build trust.** Relationships matter more than numbers.
- **Keep learning.** The world will keep changing—so must you.
- **Give value.** Money follows those who help others.
- **Stay calm.** React wisely, not emotionally.
- **Choose happiness.** Wealth is meaningless if you aren't happy.

You are on a journey, and I believe in you. The Year of the Snake is your time to grow, transform, and achieve great things. Take what I've shared, and make the most of it.

Now, go forward with wisdom—and make your dreams happen.

Your Next Step

- What's one piece of advice from this chapter that stands out to you? Write it down and start applying it today.
- If you have a lesson from your own father, mentor, or life experience, share it. Pass the wisdom forward.

The world needs more people with knowledge, patience, and heart. Be one of them

SECRET
THIRTEEN

CREATING WEALTH

THE SECRET CODE OF SUCCESS IN THE AI AGE & TIMELESS WISDOM

A PERIODICAL FOR SOCIAL MEDIA AND CONTENT CREATORS

A TRANSFORMATIONAL GUIDE TO BUILD BRAND, AND INCREASE INCOME, INFLUENCE, AND IMPACT

Secret 13 Topic: A Mother's Wisdom – Success with Heart & Balance

A Letter from Mom to Her Daughter

My dearest daughter,

Success is not just about working hard or making money—it's about living well. It's about creating something meaningful, taking care of yourself, and making a difference in people's lives.

You are strong, talented, and capable of achieving great things. But along the way, remember this: Success is not just about what you build—it's about how you live.

Here are some lessons to help you on your journey.

1. Success Means Taking Care of Yourself First

You can't pour from an empty cup. If you don't take care of yourself, how will you have the energy to create, grow, or help others?

Think of your mind and body like a garden. If you don't water the plants, they wither. If you don't pull out the weeds, they take over. **Your health, your energy, and your happiness are the foundation of everything.**

Take action:

- Get enough sleep.

- Eat food that fuels you.

- Move your body.

- Take breaks when you need them.

Don't feel guilty for resting. Rest is not wasted time—it's what keeps you going.

2. Be Kind, but Set Boundaries

Kindness is powerful. The way you treat people will shape the opportunities that come your way.

But being kind doesn't mean saying yes to everything. It doesn't mean letting people take advantage of you. **Success comes when you learn to set boundaries.**

A snake does not let others walk all over it. It moves with grace, but it knows when to defend itself.

Take action:

- Say no when something doesn't feel right.

- Protect your time and energy.

- Surround yourself with people who respect you.

You don't have to be everything to everyone. The right people will value you for who you are.

3. Trust Yourself—You Know More Than You Think

Doubt is normal. You might wonder if you're good enough, smart enough, or talented enough. But let me tell you something: **You already have what it takes.**

Too many people hold themselves back because they wait for permission. They wait for someone to say, *"You're ready."* But no one else can decide that for you.

Take action:

- Stop waiting for perfect conditions. Start now.

- If you make a mistake, learn and keep going.

- Believe in your voice, your story, and your ideas.

The people who succeed aren't the ones who never doubt themselves—they're the ones who **move forward anyway.**

4. Comparison is a Trap—Focus on Your Own Path

It's easy to look at others and feel behind. You might see someone with more followers, more money, or more success, and think, *"Why am I not there yet?"*

But comparison steals your joy. **It makes you forget how far you've come.**

A snake sheds its skin—it doesn't try to wear someone else's.

Take action:

- Celebrate your progress, no matter how small.

- Focus on your strengths, not someone else's.

- Unfollow anything that makes you feel "less than."

You are on your own journey. The only person you need to compete with is the person you were yesterday.

5. Stay Humble—Keep Learning

No matter how much success you have, **never stop learning.** The smartest people in the world are the ones who know they don't know everything.

If you think you already know it all, you stop growing. And when you stop growing, you start falling behind.

Take action:

- Listen more than you speak.

- Be open to new ideas.

- Learn from people who have walked the path before you.

Humility is not weakness—it's wisdom. **The more you learn, the stronger you become.**

6. Happiness Comes from Gratitude, Not Success

Success will not make you happy if you are always chasing the next thing. If you don't learn to appreciate what you have now, you will never feel satisfied.

Happiness is not about having more—it's about recognizing what's already enough.

Take action:

- Start each day with one thing you're grateful for.

- Celebrate small wins, not just big ones.

- Take moments to enjoy life, not just work through it.

A snake does not rush—it moves with purpose, savoring the journey.

You deserve to be happy today—not just when you reach your goal.

7. Love What You Do, or Find Something You Love

The secret to long-term success? Loving what you do.

You won't always feel motivated. There will be hard days, slow growth, and times when you feel like giving up. If you don't enjoy the process, you won't stick with it.

Take action:

- If something drains you, find a way to make it fun.

- Don't be afraid to pivot if your heart isn't in it.

- Stay curious—explore, create, and enjoy the journey.

Success is not just about making money—it's about making a life you love.

Final Words from Mother

Success is not just about hard work. It's about balance, kindness, and knowing what truly matters.

So remember this:

- **Take care of yourself.** Your health and happiness come first.

- **Set boundaries.**

- **You can be kind and still protect your time.**

- **Trust yourself.** You are more capable than you think.

- **Focus on your path.** Comparison is a waste of time.

- **Keep learning.** Growth never stops.

- **Practice gratitude.** Success means nothing without joy.

- **Enjoy the journey.** Love what you do, or change direction.

The Year of the Snake is your time to rise, grow, and succeed. Move forward with confidence, with wisdom, and with heart.

Now, go make your dreams happen. Your Next Step

- What's one lesson from this chapter that speaks to you? Write it down and start applying it today.

- If you know someone who needs encouragement, share this wisdom with them.

The world needs people who succeed with kindness, strength, and purpose. Be one of them.

CREATING WEALTH

THE SECRET CODE OF SUCCESS IN THE AI AGE & TIMELESS WISDOM

A PERIODICAL FOR SOCIAL MEDIA AND CONTENT CREATORS

A TRANSFORMATIONAL GUIDE TO BUILD BRAND, AND INCREASE INCOME, INFLUENCE, AND IMPACT

Secret 14 Topic: 14-Day Adventure to Transform Your Life: Wisdom and Strategy of the Snake

Day 1 Embracing New Beginnings

Happy New Year! Happy the Year of the Snake, Chinese New Year, or Spring Festival, is one of the most important traditions for us. It symbolizes reunion, hope, and new beginnings. At this special moment, I want to share a heartfelt message with you, hoping it brings you inspiration and warmth. This year, January 29 marks the Chinese New Year—a festival to reflect on the past and embrace the future. It's a time to come home, reunite, and reignite our dreams. In this fast-changing world, technology has brought us closer, but our hearts need even deeper connections. Music is a magical language—no borders or barriers. Whether it's joy or sorrow, a melody can bring you and me closer together. Music brings love and hope; it reminds us of the beauty of our shared humanity.

Today, as we stand at the beginning of a new year, let us not only celebrate the achievements of the past but also embrace the opportunities of the future. Let's use kindness and love to sow seeds of goodness in this world. Every small act of goodness contributes to the greater picture, just like the lanterns during the Spring Festival—no matter how small the light, it brightens the darkness. Just as the mission of my books, Success in Music Made Simple, Music Festival in AI Age， Sparkfire, Art, Wealth, and Success.

I truly believe that music and love can unite us. Through music, we can hear each other's stories and feel the beauty of different cultures. Let us connect through melodies, act with purpose, and make the world a warmer and more inclusive place.

My friends, let's strive to be the best version of ourselves this year. Cherish those around you, live with gratitude, and let music be the bond, love be the belief, as we work together to build a brighter future.

Wishing you all a Happy Chinese New Year! Happy the Year of the Snake! May your family be blessed with happiness, health, and success. Thank you for your support, and I'll see you tomorrow!

Day 2 Welcoming the Year of the Snake & the Joy of the Spring Festival

Hello, Everyone!

Today, I'm excited to introduce you to one of the most cherished and vibrant celebrations in Chinese culture—the Spring Festival, also known as Chinese New Year. This festival marks the beginning of a new year on the traditional lunisolar calendar and celebrates the transition from winter to spring.

The Spring Festival lasts from Chinese New Year's Eve to the Lantern Festival, and it's a time filled with joy, tradition, and family. Families come together for reunion dinners, decorate their homes with red symbols of good fortune, and light firecrackers to welcome a fresh start. Homes are cleaned to sweep away ill fortune, making way for good luck, and red envelopes filled with blessings are exchanged to spread happiness and prosperity.

Now, here's something fun you can learn: In Mandarin, we say "Happy Chinese New Year" as 新年快乐 (Xīn Nián Kuài Lè)!

Xīn Nián (新年) means "New Year."

Kuài Lè (快乐) means "Happy."

Let's say it together: Xīn Nián Kuài Lè! Great job!

The Spring Festival is not just about tradition—it's about embracing new beginnings, cherishing loved ones, and spreading hope for a brighter future. Wherever you are in the world, let's carry this message of renewal, positivity, and togetherness into the year ahead. Wishing you all a happy New Year and a year filled with love, joy, and success. Happy the Year of Snake. Thank you for watching, and I'll see you tomorrow!

119

Day 3 Wisdom and Transformation

Hello everyone, Welcome to the Year of the Snake!

As we enter this new year, we welcome the energy of the Snake, a symbol of wisdom, transformation, and perseverance. The snake moves forward with grace and strategy, reminding us to embrace change, trust our instincts, and approach challenges with intelligence.

In Chinese culture, the Year of the Snake is associated with deep thinking, resilience, and new beginnings. Just like a snake shedding its old skin, this is a time to release the past and step into a future filled with growth and opportunity. Whether it's in your career, relationships, or personal goals, this is the perfect time to reinvent yourself and embrace new possibilities.

May this year bring you wisdom to make the right choices, strength to overcome obstacles, and success in all that you pursue.

Wishing you a joyful and prosperous Year of the Snake!

In Mandarin, we say: 新年快乐 (Xīn Nián Kuài Lè) – Happy New Year!

Or 蛇年大吉 (Shé Nián Dà Jí) – Wishing you great fortune in the Year of the Snake!

May this year be filled with happiness, health, and endless possibilities. Let's move forward with hope and determination!

新年快乐，蛇年幸福！

Chuntianle (New Power Art)

chuntianlec@gmail.com

Spring
IMPRESSION

Day 4. The Wisdom of Knowing When to Stop. The Story of "Adding Feet to a Snake" (画蛇添足)

Hello, everyone,

The Year of the Snake is a time of wisdom and reflection. One famous Chinese story teaches us an important lesson about knowing when to stop—the story of "Adding Feet to a Snake."This tale comes from the Warring States Strategies (战国策), a collection of political and military stories from ancient China. In the story, a strategist warns a prime minister about overreaching ambition, using the metaphor of a man who ruins his success by adding unnecessary activity—just like giving feet to a snake.

Long ago, in the state of Chu, a family held an ancestral ceremony. After the ritual, they had a pot of wine left and wanted to reward the helpers. But there was a problem—there was only enough wine for one person to drink fully. To decide who would get the wine, someone suggested a game: "Let's each draw a snake on the ground. Whoever finishes first will win the wine." Everyone agreed, and the competition began.

One man quickly finished drawing his snake. Seeing that others were still drawing, he felt proud and thought, I am so fast! I have time to add feet to my snake! Holding the wine pot in one hand, he used the other to draw extra feet on his snake. But just before he finished, another man completed his snake.

The second man grabbed the wine and said, "Snakes don't have feet! You ruined your drawing. The real winner is me."

With that, he drank the wine, leaving the first man empty-handed.

The Meaning of the Story. This story teaches us that doing extra does not always mean doing better. The man had already won, but by trying to show off, he lost everything. The idiom "Adding Feet to a Snake" (画蛇添足) warns us against unnecessary actions that can ruin success. It reminds us to be wise, stay focused, and know when to stop.

Day 5. Overcoming Fear—The Illusion of the Snake, The Story of "Seeing a Snake in the Cup" (杯弓蛇影)

One day, he prepared a big feast for his friends. The guests were happily drinking and chatting when one of them noticed something strange. As he lifted his cup to drink, he saw a small snake-like shadow moving inside his drink. He felt disgusted and scared, but he didn't want to offend his host. So, he forced himself to drink it, pretending everything was fine. However, as soon as he left the party, he felt sick. He couldn't stop thinking about the snake in his cup.

SEEING A SNAKE IN THE CUP

The fear grew stronger each day. He convinced himself that he had swallowed a real snake. Soon, he became very ill and stopped visiting Guang Le. Guang Le noticed his friend's absence and decided to check on him. When he arrived, he found

124

his friend lying in bed, looking weak and pale. "What happened? You were fine at the party!" Guang Le asked. The sick man hesitated but finally confessed: "I saw a snake in my wine that night. I was too polite to refuse the drink, but after that, I've felt like the snake is inside me. I can't eat, sleep, or think about anything else. I know I am sick because of it."

Guang Le thought for a moment, then suddenly realized the truth. He remembered that a painted bow was hanging on the wall where his friend had been sitting. The snake in the cup was actually just the reflection of the bow! To prove this, he invited his friend back to his house. He poured a cup of drink and asked the man to hold it in the same spot. The same snake-like shadow appeared in the cup! Guang Le laughed and pointed at the bow on the wall. "Look! The snake you saw was just the reflection of this bow. You never drank a snake!" His friend finally understood. His fear was all in his mind. The relief washed over him, and he quickly recovered.

The Lesson of the Story. This story teaches you that fear and worry can sometimes be illusions. When you let your imagination run wild, it can make you sick or anxious. Instead, you should seek the truth before letting fear control you. In the Year of the Snake, let's remember to stay calm, think clearly, and not let imaginary fears stop you from enjoying life. Thank you.

Day 6 "Startling the Snake by Striking the Grass" – A Lesson in Caution and Strategy (打草惊蛇)

The Year of the Snake: The Story of "Startling the Snake by Striking the Grass". Hello everyone, in the Year of the Snake, let's reflect on caution and unintended consequences. A famous Chinese idiom, "Startling the Snake by Striking the Grass" (打草惊蛇), teaches you the importance of being discreet. This story in Northern Song Dynasty comes from the Southern Tang period during the Five Dynasties. In a place called Dangtu County (now part of Anhui, China), there was a corrupt official named Wang Lu. He cared only about wealth, taking bribes and ignoring justice. Under his rule, the local officials followed his example, openly abusing their power and exploiting the people. The citizens suffered greatly and longed for justice.

126

Startling
the Snake
by stricking the grass

One day, a young man had a dispute with his neighbor over land. The argument escalated, and they decided to take the matter to court. However, when they arrived at the county office, the guards refused to let them in unless they paid a bribe. The young man reluctantly gave some money and was finally allowed inside. But before he could speak to the magistrate, the court secretary blocked his way. Recognizing the secretary, the neighbor quickly handed him a silver ingot and whispered, "It's my land, please help me." The secretary smiled and turned to the young man, scolding, "Such a small matter! How dare you

127

disturb the magistrate? Get out!" With no choice, the young man was thrown out of the court.

Angry and frustrated, he gathered others who had suffered similar injustices. Together, they wrote a formal complaint against the corrupt secretary and submitted it to the magistrate, Wang Lu. When Wang Lu read the document, he panicked. The complaint described the secretary's corruption in detail—many of these crimes were done under Wang Lu's orders. If investigated, he himself would be exposed. Fortunately, the complaint had first reached his hands, giving him time to cover up his crimes. To avoid further trouble, he dismissed the case and wrote on the document:"You may have struck the grass, but I, the snake, have already been startled."This meant that although they had accused his subordinate, he had realized the danger and would now be more cautious.

The Lesson of the Story. This story teaches you that people who do wrong are often the most fearful. Even the slightest threat can make them panic. It also reminds you to act wisely—if we are too direct in exposing corruption or deception, you may alert the wrongdoers before justice can be served. In the Year of the Snake, let's learn from this story and be thoughtful in your actions. Thank you.

Day 7 Tiger's Head, Snake's Tail - The Importance of Finishing Strong (虎头蛇尾)

The year of the snake: The Story of "Tiger's Head, Snake's Tail". Hello everyone, As we welcome the Year of the Snake, let's reflect on an important lesson about perseverance and consistency. There is an old Chinese idiom, "Tiger's Head, Snake's Tail" (虎头蛇尾, hǔ tóu shé wěi), which describes something that starts strong but ends weakly. It warns us against losing momentum and giving up at the halfway. There are different stories about this idiom, this is one of them.

A long time ago, during the Qing Dynasty, government corruption was widespread. Many officials were chosen based on connections rather than ability. Talented scholars without the right connections struggled to find opportunities, while those with wealth and influence could buy their way into power.

One day, a senior government official in the capital proposed a reform. He suggested that all officials should be tested on their knowledge and skills to ensure that only the most capable remained in power. The emperor approved this idea, and soon, the governor of Hunan received the order to organize the exam. On exam day, the governor personally oversaw the event. Suddenly, a man was caught taking the test for someone else. Furious, the governor declared, "Impersonation is a crime! He must be punished!" Officials gathered, expecting swift justice.

But as time passed, nothing happened. They soon learned that the impersonator was a relative of the governor. To avoid scandal, the case was quietly dropped. The exam system, meant to bring fairness, became meaningless.

This is the perfect example of "Tiger's Head, Snake's Tail"—a strong and ambitious beginning, but a weak and disappointing ending.

The Lesson of the story. Success isn't just about starting with passion and energy; it's about finishing what you begin. Whether in studies, work, or personal goals, persistence is the key. The Year of the Snake reminds us: don't let your efforts fade away like a snake's tail—finish what you start! Thank you.

Day 8 The Snake That Tries to Swallow an Elephant – A Lesson on Greed (蛇吞象)

The Year of the Snake: The snake that tries to swallow an elephant. Hello, everyone, welcome to the Year of the Snake! This year, let's reflect on a valuable lesson about greed and knowing one's limits. There is an old saying in China: "The snake that tries to swallow an elephant" (蛇吞象, shé tūn xiàng). It warns against excessive greed—want too much and lose everything in the process.

Here's a story to help you understand this wisdom.

A long time ago, deep in the mountains, there lived a snake named Jiao. He was not the largest snake, but he was clever and ambitious. Jiao always wanted more—more food, more land, and more power.

131

One day, he moved through the forest and saw a big boar. "If I can eat this boar, I will be the strongest of all snakes!" he thought. Jiao attacked, wrapping his body around the boar. But the boar was too big, and no matter how hard he tried, Jiao couldn't swallow it. Still, he refused to give up.

Days passed, and Jiao grew weaker. But his greed was stronger than his hunger. Then, he saw something even bigger—an elephant drinking by the river. "If I can swallow the elephant, I will be feared by all!" he thought. Ignoring his failing strength, Jiao lunged at the elephant.

The elephant barely noticed. With one step, it crushed Jiao's tail. The once-proud snake now lay helpless, trapped by his own greed. Unable to move, he soon became prey for the very animals he had once hunted.

The Lesson of the story: Greed blinds you to reality. Wanting too much can lead to your downfall. In this Year of the Snake, remember: Be ambitious, but know your limits. Be wise, not reckless. Thank you.

Day 9 Rise Like the Soaring Snake – Riding the Wind of Opportunity (腾蛇成风)

Rise Like the Soaring Snake – Embracing Opportunity in the Year of the Snake. Hello everyone, As you step into the Year of the Snake, think about what this symbol means. The snake moves with grace, patience, and strategy. It doesn't rush, but when the moment is right, it strikes with precision. There is an idiom, "The soaring snake rides the wind", you can view it as the meaning that with the right timing and opportunity, you can rise higher than you ever imagined.

Success isn't just about working hard—it's about working smart. Like a snake sensing the right moment to move, you must learn to recognize opportunities and act when the time is right. Many people spend years working tirelessly but remain stuck because they don't adapt to change. The snake teaches you to be flexible, observant, and ready to seize the moment.

Think about your own goals. Maybe you want to improve in your career, start a new project, or improve your skills. The world is always changing, and if you wait for the perfect time, you may never start. Instead, be like the snake—stay aware, trust your instincts, and move forward when the chance appears.

However, remember that success doesn't come from a single lucky moment. Even the fastest snake moves with patience and strategy. You must prepare, build your skills, and position yourself for the right opportunity. Luck favors those who are ready.

This year, challenge yourself to embrace change. If an opportunity comes, don't hesitate. If you face obstacles, don't fear them—adapt, just as the snake does. With focus and determination, you can rise higher than you ever thought possible.

The Year of the Snake is your time to move forward. Stay sharp, stay patient, and when the moment is right—strike!

Thank you.

Day 10 The Hidden Snake in the Grass – Patience and Precision for Success (蛇伏于草)

Success in the Year of the Snake: Stay Low, Strike High. Hello everyone, As you step into the Year of the Snake, think about how a snake moves. It doesn't rush. It waits, observes, and when the time is right, it strikes with precision. "A snake hides in the grass", meaning those with wisdom stay patient, build their strength, and act at the right moment.

In life, success isn't about being the loudest or the fastest. It's about knowing when to move. Some people rush into opportunities without preparation, only to fail quickly. Others, like the snake, take time to learn, improve, and prepare. When the perfect moment arrives, they are ready to act and succeed in one bold move.

135

But remember—waiting is not doing nothing. A snake in the grass is not asleep—it is watching, learning, and preparing. You should do the same. While you wait for the right opportunity, keep making progress. Every day, take action toward your goal. Improve your skills, expand your knowledge, and strengthen your mind. The effort you put in now will determine your success later.

Think about your own journey. Maybe you want to start a business, advance in your career, or master a skill. If you try too soon, without enough preparation, you might struggle. But if you take time to build your foundation, success will come naturally.

The Year of the Snake teaches patience and strategy. Stay calm, keep moving forward, and when the time is right—strike with confidence.

This is your year. Make every moment count.

Thank you.

Day 11. From Snake to Dragon: Embrace Growth and Transformation (蛇化为龙)

The Year of the Snake: Grow, Transform, and Rise.The snake can turn into a dragon。 Hello everyone, As you step into the Year of the Snake, think about the power of transformation. "The snake can turn into a dragon." This means that through continuous effort, growth, and learning, you can achieve great success. Just like a snake sheds its skin to grow, you, too, can evolve into a stronger and wiser version of yourself.

Embrace Change and Keep Learning

A snake doesn't stay the same; it constantly sheds its skin. This is a reminder that growth requires letting go of old habits, fears, and limitations. If you want to achieve something great, you must be willing to learn new skills and adapt to change. Whether it's improving your career, mastering a new skill, or building better relationships, growth starts with small, consistent efforts.

Be Patient, but Keep Moving

A snake knows when to stay still and when to strike. Patience is important, but waiting does not mean doing nothing. While waiting for the right opportunity, you must keep learning, preparing, and improving. Every small step you take brings you closer to your goal. Success is not about rushing—it's about moving forward wisely.

Turn Challenges into Strength

Life is full of challenges, but just like a snake uses its flexibility to navigate obstacles, you can use your experiences—both good and bad—to grow stronger. Instead of fearing difficulties, see them as stepping stones to success. Every challenge you overcome makes you more resilient and prepared for bigger opportunities.

Believe in Your Own Transformation

The snake starts small, but with time, effort, and persistence, it transforms. You have that same potential. No matter where you are now, you can rise higher. Stay focused, keep improving, and never stop believing in your ability to grow.

In the Year of the Snake, embrace change, stay patient, and work towards your goals. With determination, you, too, can transform and rise like a dragon. Happy Year of the Snake! May this year bring you growth, success, and new beginnings!

Day 12 Walk Like a Snake, Step Like a Dragon: Success Through Steady Progress. (蛇行龙步)

The Year of the Snake: Move Steadily, Win Surely. Walk like a snake, step like a dragon. Hello everyone, As you enter the Year of the Snake, think about how you move through life. "Walk as a Snake, step as a Dragon." This means success comes from steady and strategic progress. In a world full of uncertainty, your ability to adapt and move wisely will determine your success.

Stay Flexible but Steady. A snake moves with grace and precision. It does not rush, but it never stops. Success is the same. You don't have to be the fastest, but you must keep moving forward. Stay flexible in your approach, but firm in your direction. When challenges come, don't panic—adjust and keep going.

Think Before You Act. A snake never strikes without careful observation. It waits for the right moment. In life, rushing into decisions without thinking can lead to failure. Whether in your career, relationships, or personal goals, take time to assess your options. Make smart, well-thought-out moves, and you will always be one step ahead.

Small Steps Lead to Big Wins. You don't need to make giant leaps to be successful. Even the smallest steps, taken consistently, lead to great achievements. Every skill you build, every lesson you learn, and every challenge you overcome adds up. Stay patient, stay focused, and keep progressing—one step at a time.

Stay Calm in Uncertain Times. The world is always changing, and unexpected challenges will arise. A snake moves smoothly, even on rough terrain. When life gets tough, don't let fear or doubt stop you. Trust yourself, adapt to the situation, and keep moving forward. Stability comes from confidence and preparation.

Your Victory is Built Daily. Success is not about one big moment—it's about the steps you take every day. Be mindful of your actions, stay disciplined, and don't lose focus. If you keep moving wisely, victory is only a matter of time.

This Year of the Snake, walk steadily, think strategically, and keep growing. Step by step, you are on your way to success. Wishing you a year of progress, strength, and achievement! Thank you.

Day 13_The Way of the Soaring Snake: Wisdom, Strategy, and Transformation. (腾蛇之道)

The Year of the Snake: Wisdom from the Past, Success for the Future. Hello everyone, this is Chuntianle.As you step into the Year of the Snake, take a moment to reflect on what this symbol means. In Chinese culture, the snake represents wisdom, adaptability, patience, and transformation. It moves with purpose, waits for the right moment, and strikes with precision. These qualities are not just ancient symbols—they are powerful lessons you can apply to your own journey.

Go with the Flow, but Stay in Control. A snake does not fight against the current. It moves with the wind, adapts to its surroundings, and finds the best path forward. In life, you will face challenges and unexpected changes. Instead of resisting, learn to adjust. Success comes from recognizing opportunities and making the best use of what is in front of you. Stay flexible, but never lose sight of your goal.

Build Your Strength in Silence. A snake does not rush into action. It hides, observes, and prepares. In the same way, your success does not come overnight. Every skill you develop, every piece of knowledge you gain, and every challenge you overcome adds to your strength. Even if no one notices your hard work now, it will pay off when the time is right. Waiting does not mean doing nothing. Use this time to sharpen your skills, build your confidence, and stay ready. When the right moment comes, you will be unstoppable.

Strike with Precision. A snake does not waste energy. It does not chase after every opportunity—it waits for the perfect one. In life, don't be distracted by every trend or shortcut. Focus on what truly matters. When you act, do it with confidence and purpose. One well-planned move is worth more than a hundred rushed decisions.

Embrace Change and Transformation. A snake sheds its skin to grow. This reminds you that change is a natural and necessary part of life. Holding onto the past, fearing new opportunities, or staying in your comfort zone will only hold you back. If you want to succeed, be willing to let go of old habits, embrace new challenges, and reinvent yourself when needed.

Your Path to Success. This Year of the Snake, move wisely. Adapt when needed, prepare in silence, and act with precision. Keep learning, keep improving, and trust that your moment to shine will come. Wishing you wisdom, strength, and success in the Year of the Snake! Thank you.

Day 14 The White Snake's Love: Growth, Devotion, and Transformation (白蛇传)

Happy Valentine's Day Special – The Snake and Love. Hello, my friend! Happy Valentine's Day! Today, let's talk about something unexpected—snakes and love. You might wonder, what do snakes have to do with love? More than you think! Snakes have fascinated people for centuries. Some fear them, while others admire their mystery and transformation. But what if I told you that a snake could teach you something about love?

Think about how a snake sheds its skin. It grows and changes, letting go of the old to embrace something new. Love is like that, too. When you truly love someone, you grow together. You learn to let go of past mistakes, misunderstandings, and fears. You become a better version of yourself, just like the snake becoming stronger after shedding its old skin.

In ancient Chinese mythology, there is a famous story called The Legend of the White Snake. It tells of a beautiful snake spirit who transforms into a woman and falls in love with a kind scholar. Their love is tested by society, fate, and even powerful forces that try to keep them apart. But the White Snake never gives up. She fights for her love, proving that true love is about devotion, courage, and never letting go.

Maybe you've been hurt before. Maybe love feels like a risk you don't want to take again. But love, like a snake, is persistent. It finds its way through cracks, moving forward no matter what stands in the way. Sometimes, love is gentle and warm like the sun on a spring morning. Other times, it is fierce, like a storm that shakes your world. But no matter what form it takes, love has the power to transform you.

You may have heard that snakes symbolize temptation. But they also represent wisdom and healing. Love, too, has this duality. It can make you feel vulnerable, but it can also make you strong. Love teaches you patience, understanding, and resilience.

This Valentine's Day, don't be afraid to open your heart. Love is not just about romance. It's in the small moments—kindness to a friend, laughter with family, appreciation for the beauty around you. It's in the courage to forgive and the strength to keep going.

So, my friend, embrace love like a snake embracing the earth— strong, fearless, and full of life. Shed your doubts, let love in, and allow it to transform you. Happy Valentine's Day! Thank you.

CREATING WEALTH

THE SECRET CODE OF SUCCESS IN THE AI AGE & TIMELESS WISDOM

A PERIODICAL FOR SOCIAL MEDIA AND CONTENT CREATORS

A TRANSFORMATIONAL GUIDE TO BUILD BRAND, AND INCREASE INCOME, INFLUENCE, AND IMPACT

Secret 15 The Twelve Zodiac Signs - A Timeless Reference:

Many people are particularly curious about the order of the twelve zodiac signs. In fact, everyone knows that each person's zodiac sign is determined by the year and month of birth, and people wonder why there are 12 zodiac signs to represent our zodiac signs, after all, there are so many animals. Then let the editor of the perpetual calendar tell you about the order of the twelve zodiac signs!

1. The order of the twelve zodiac signs

1.子鼠	Rat (ZǐShǔ)
2.丑牛	Ox (Chǒu Niú)
3.寅虎	Tiger (Yín Hǔ)
4.卯兔	Rabbit (Mǎo Tù)
5.辰龙	Dragon (Chén Lóng)
6.巳蛇	Snake (SìShé)
7.午马	Horse (WǔMǎ)
8.未羊	Sheep (Wèi Yáng)
9.申猴	Monkey (Shēn Hóu)
10.酉鸡	Rooster (Yǒu Jī)
11.戌狗	Dog (XūGǒu)
12.亥猪	Pig (Hài Zhū)

2. The relationship between natural phenomena and animal habits:

1) Zishi (midnight, about 11 to 1 a.m.), when the world is in chaos, mice are most active, so it is called "Zi Rat";

2) Choushi (cock crowing, about 1 to 3 a.m.), cows begin to ruminate at this time, symbolizing the beginning of agricultural civilization, "Chou Cow";

3) Yinshi (dawn, about 3 to 5 a.m.), tigers are active frequently, symbolizing bravery and majesty, "Yin Tiger";

4) Maoshi (sunrise, about 5 to 7 a.m.), rabbits are mostly active at dawn, "Mao Rabbit";

5) Chenshi (food time, about 7 to 9 a.m.), dragons are in charge of rain in mythology and legends, and this is when rain moistens the earth, "Chen Dragon";

6) Sishi (midnight, about 9 to 11 a.m.), snakes like to appear in the warm sunshine, "Si Snake" ;

7) Wushi (midday, about 11 am to 1 pm), horses can still gallop under the scorching sun, symbolizing the peak of Yang energy, "Wu horse";

8) Weishi (sunset, about 1 pm to 3 pm), it is suitable for sheep to graze at this time, and "Wei" belongs to the earth element, which is consistent with the gentle and stable temperament of sheep, "Wei sheep";

9) Shenshi (sunset, about 3 pm to 5 pm), monkeys are particularly active around dusk, "Shen monkey";

147

10) Youshi (sunset, about 5 pm to 7 pm), at this time, chickens return to the nest to tell the time, "You chicken";

11) Xushi (dusk, about 7 pm to 9 pm), dogs begin to guard the house, "Xu dog";

12) Haishi (dawn, about 9 pm to 11 pm), pigs are used to resting at night, and the ancients believed that Haishi was heavy in moisture, which was consistent with the image of pigs, "Hai pig".

3. Comparison table of the twelve zodiac signs by year

Zodiac sign	Year of birth
Rat	1948, 1960, 1972, 1984, 1996, 2008, 2020
Ox	1949, 1961, 1973, 1985, 1997, 2009, 2021
Tiger	1950, 1962, 1974, 1986, 1998, 2010, 2022
Rabbit	1951, 1963, 1975, 1987, 1999, 2011, 2023
Dragon	1952, 1964, 1976, 1988, 2000, 2012, 2024
Snake|	1953, 1965, 1977, 1989, 2001, 2013, 2025
Horse		1954, 1966, 1978, 1990, 2002, 2014, 2026
Goat|	1955, 1967, 1979, 1991, 2003, 2015, 2027
Monkey	1956, 1968, 1980, 1992, 2004, 2016, 2028
Rooster	1957, 1969, 1981, 1993, 2005, 2017, 2029
Dog	1958, 1970, 1982, 1994, 2006, 2018, 2030
Pig	1959, 1971, 1983, 1995, 2007, 2019, 2031

CREATING WEALTH

THE SECRET CODE OF SUCCESS IN THE AI AGE & TIMELESS WISDOM

A PERIODICAL FOR SOCIAL MEDIA AND CONTENT CREATORS

A TRANSFORMATIONAL GUIDE TO BUILD BRAND, AND INCREASE INCOME, INFLUENCE, AND IMPACT

Secret 16 Portraits of Life: Stories That Shape Us

Life's Insights Jing W.（P.R.China）

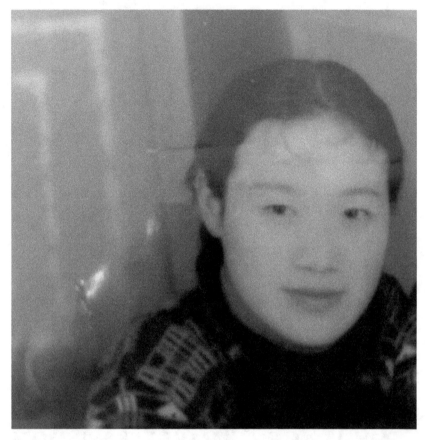

At the beginning of the new year, everything is renewed. The Year of the Snake in 2025 has arrived as scheduled. I wish you and I can live like a snake, with more wisdom and more opportunities.

I am already in my fifty, and I always encourage myself with an optimistic and open-minded attitude. Because of many

150

experiences in life, sadness sometimes comes out, sighing that the years pass too quickly, complaining that fate has caused some problems with my health, that time is really not durable, and that I have been confused for half of my life. It feels like being young is a very distant thing, but the sun rises and sets, and the flowers bloom and fade. Who can go against such a natural law? When you are young, you are confused, excited, regretful, and struggling. You have to accept yourself at each stage. Because this is life. Everyone will be anxious, but you have to heal yourself. Everyone has worries, but you have to digest them yourself. With the increase of age, mature mind, people and things around you, everything will be relieved.

In 2025, live a good life and bloom all the way. I only hope that you and I are well. Make peace with everything and be at peace with being alone. May every year bring this joy, and every day be as wonderful as today.

Chuntianle (New Power Art)

chuntianlec@gmail.com

Spring
IMPRESSION

Beautiful Year of the Snake, Liu Ling (P.R. China)

In ancient China, people regarded snakes as symbols of mystery, wisdom and spirituality, and associated them with dragons, calling them "little dragons". Snakes symbolize change, regeneration, and tenacious vitality. The Year of the Snake is full of development opportunities and change, so opportunities should be seized in this year. As the saying goes, "You can see the head of the dragon but not the tail", and snakes symbolize alertness and change in Chinese culture.

I plan to ride from Xi'an to the East China Sea in the bright spring, and ride from Shandong to the Sino-North Korean border along the beautiful coast. The sea is like our hometown, warming our inner world. Feel the great mountains and rivers of the motherland up close, the spectacular scenery is more beautiful than poetry!

The azure blue sea has the misty fairyland of Penglai, and appreciates the magnificent mountains and rivers described in the "Classic of Mountains and Seas" closely. I hope to exercise my body and self-will through cycling, chase the distant stars and the sea, and find the distant poetry and the true meaning of life in the trivial daily life.

Chuntianle (New Power Art)

chuntianlec@gmail.com

Spring Impression

SEVENTEEN

CREATING WEALTH

THE SECRET CODE OF SUCCESS IN THE AI AGE & TIMELESS WISDOM

A PERIODICAL FOR SOCIAL MEDIA AND CONTENT CREATORS

A TRANSFORMATIONAL GUIDE TO BUILD BRAND, AND INCREASE INCOME, INFLUENCE, AND IMPACT

Secret 17 Homeland of Emerging Social Medial and Content Creators

Spring is here! Announcing the International Spring Impression Event!

4th International Event – Spring Impression (March 2025)

The Year of the Snake inspires me, and your support encourages me. I'm excited to announce our event in March 2025. The Year of the Snake – Art, Wealth, and Success: A Periodical Book for Emerging Social Media and Content Creators. This revolutionary guide is designed to help artists and creators like you to build wealth, establish a strong brand, and thrive in the modern creative landscape.

This program will inspire readers all over the world and highlight its impact on emerging artists and creators. Same goal as our periodical book "Sparkfire - Art, Wealth, and Success".

• A Revolutionary Guide to Increase Your Influence, Income, and Impact

• Practical strategies to increase your success, build wealth, and create a lasting brand.

• Insights into leveraging AI, exploring Chinese cultural wisdom, and understanding multiple income streams for creative growth.

Also, same mission as our book "Success in Music Made Simple", "The Music Festival in AI Age", Let's unite Eastern and Western art to create a better world.

Dear friends, in the beautiful springtime, it is time to embrace the beauty of the world, and showcase yourself, your talents in music, cuisine, martial arts, or any form of artistry, and share the message to the world.

The Event will be launched roughly in March 2025, so mark your calendars! Submissions are open until Feb. 20. Send a request to the email on the screen and leave the comments to share your voice.

I believe our program could become a powerful resource for artists and creators around the world. Don't miss this opportunity to shine! Thank you.

Ludwig (Germany)

Hello, my name is Ludwig, I am a guitar player from Germany and have been playing in a surfrock band in my teenage years, which brought me a great deal of joy. Unfortunately, due to family and work commitments, I later found less time for my hobby. Today, although I should actually be retired, (but I am still working full-time alongside YouTube), I have rediscovered the time and passion for my beloved guitar since 2020.

I have never given up on my dreams and still want to share my passion with the world.

My message for you: Follow your dreams, pursue your passion, and never give up!

If you'd like to follow my musical journey, feel free to check out

my YouTube channel: youtube.com/ludwigguitar.

Chuntianle (New Power Art)

chuntianlec@gmail.com

Spring Impression

Debrydelys Deeberdeyn (Switzerland)

Talking about the Year of the Snake. . . Here's a big and intriguing surprise that I didn't expect. Every invitation I receive from every part of the world is always a surprise, I receive many, but being here again with Chuntianle always represents a celebration, in my heart and in my working days.

Many people have already contacted me asking "Debrydelys, what will you talk about in the new Chuntianle book"? Or "Debrydelys, do you have any advice for us"?

Even for a person like me, a European, who didn't know much about these topics before, can feel fascinated by an invitation of this kind; there is a world to discover out there and we must not miss the opportunity. There are many things to say I also often ask myself "what can I give to the world, and what can I really give"? Of course, even an artist asks himself questions of this kind, especially in private. All the displays of affection, recognition, compliments, gifts, everything that I receive from the world makes me think that my activity as an artist is appreciated, often much more than I would have thought at the beginning.

But we all know well that in our lives our commitment never ends. We still have so much to offer.

Thanks to this splendid writer, Chuntianle, I had the opportunity to find out more closely about the meaning of the Year of the Snake, as I am usually used to reading the zodiac as it is seen in Western countries. When I think about my past life I must admit that my personal path actually corresponds enormously to the typical characteristics described and recognized as belonging to the sign of those born in the years of the snake. And I discovered that I too was born in one of these years.

Personally, I have always sought renewal, spirituality, change, evolution. I have felt these internal needs since I was a child. Looking back I clearly see that I was looking for exactly this, a new rebirth along with many other rebirths. Many things ended, I know, but many others were born later. And I continue to hope, to search, to create new births in new paths, which can also arise from paths that I did not know before. I have learned to accept many new things, unexplored dimensions that I once didn't even think I would encounter on my path, yet they presented themselves.

The forecast offers an interesting look for this Year of the Snake, and therefore I must keep myself ready and well prepared for any eventuality. There are already some signs that make me think of a challenging year, where I hope to offer the best of myself. It's not easy, but it's never been easy before either, I have to work a lot, and in many different artistic sectors, considering the numerous requests I receive, but precisely these predictions push me to be more proactive. Isn't the fact that I'm still here with Chuntianle already a telltale sign of particular interest?

Naturally, it is up to each of us to know how to accept the proposals that destiny wants to make to us and if we are more available and more open to the new opportunities that present themselves to us in this new year we will reap considerable satisfaction.

An open mind, a mind that embraces intuitions, suggestions, transformations, combining the fundamental characteristics typical of the Western and Eastern worlds, can know and experience states of mind that perhaps they had not imagined before.

For this year I recommend dedicating yourself to constructive pastimes, such as painting, dancing, yoga, walking in the countryside, and more, and to cut away from the negative or toxic relationships that stop our creativity. The snake sheds its skin. . . maybe we will change it too.

FR3DROQ MUSIC (USA)

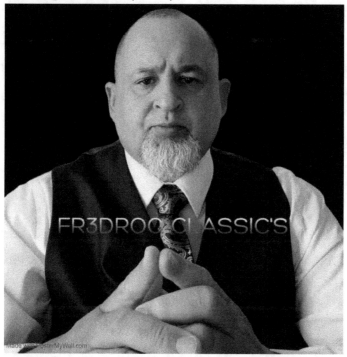

FR3DROQ MUSIC FROM THE US

- 2024 PRODUCED OVER 10 ALBUMS WITH VARIOUS ARTISTS
- WAS GUEST ON 3 DIFFERENT PODCASTS
- I WORK CURRENTLY WITH 5 ARTISTS

- WAS PART OF THE NEW POWER OF ART BOOK IN 2024
- ENJOY WORKING WITH DIFFERENT GENERES AND NEW ARTISTS
- RELEASED NEW SOLO PROJECT IN 2/2025
- HAVE BEEN PLAYING MUSIC SINCE A KIDSTARTED OUT A DRUMMER/PERCUSSIONIST

Paul Devine Music (USA)

Since I was a boy, music was my therapy. My parents had divorced, and I had gone to live with my father. My Dad was a great Dad, but whenever I missed my mom, I would sit down at the piano and pick out some chords. I grew to learn to play the piano by ear, and whenever I felt sad, music would drown out the sadness. And I know just as music touched my life, it can touch and help other people's lives all over the world. This is my personal vision for the future, and I am very thankful to God for that.

Piano Matron Nee Nee (USA)
Year of the Snake 2025

The Year of the Snake represents transformation, patience, wisdom, intuition, purpose and instinct. It's a time to embrace the unknown, and seize the opportunity for growth. As we welcome the 2025 Year of the Snake, it's a time to reflect. Sometimes in life, something catastrophic happens that forces one to start a different path.

And while times can be challenging and tough, like the Snake, we are determined to adapt to those difficult situations.

It was 2013 (The Year of the Snake). While vacationing in California, I severely broke my leg. For the next several months, I'd spend most days, confined to the couch, unable to walk, with little to do. Boredom set in, and I passed time by doing motionless activities like reading, watching TV and doing countless crossword puzzles. After several weeks, I went back to my orthopedic surgeon for a follow up. Sadly he informed me,

"You leg isn't healing properly.". I would spend the next several months immobilized on the couch, the worst news I could possibly hear. I was completely shattered.

I spent the next few days processing the news, trying to figure out how to cope. Like the Snake, it was my time to adapt to the situation and do something productive, challenging and purpose-driven. It was then, I purchased my first piano keyboard. I spent the next few months practicing religiously. I'd spend hours and hours educating myself on learning the piano. I eagerly purchased all the piano books I could get my hands on, watched countless videos, patiently learned scales, chords, fingerings and everything else I could about the piano. I then learned my very first piece, Fur Elise by Beethoven.

Reflecting back, had I not broken my leg so severely, I would have never had the patience or time to learn the piano. In addition, by breaking my leg, not only did it encourage me to learn piano, it also led me to a major career change. I had the honor to teach Chinese students English! Throughout my years as an English teacher, I taught tens of thousands of students, many of which I'm still close to today. It was an honor to watch them grow and excel. I've heard their stories, met their families and shared in their culture. Before retiring last year, I received an award for top 10% of all teachers. It's a privilege knowing I made a difference in their lives. And like playing piano, it all started by breaking my leg.

Sandra Holzer-Vieider (Italy)

Our Theater Group is so happy today to be invited and say a few words regarding this fascinating theme of the Year of the Snake. To many in Europe, it seems like something new that has arrived a few years ago, from distant exotic countries. And so China managed to conquer us too.

After reading the interesting publication "Sparkfire Art Wealth and Success", and after the invitation received from the actor Debrydelys Deeberdeyn, a dear colleague we met many times on film sets, we met Chuntianle, and we didn't have to ask too much to take part in this wonderful periodic project.

What do we expect from this magical year? So many beautiful and overwhelming things. Yes, even if we have many difficulties in our theatrical works, especially of a financial nature, we hope that our projects can continue and achieve the success we hope for.

But this is the year that China considers so special for people who want to look forward and build a brighter future, despite the obstacles. until a few years ago, here in Europe this topic was very little known, but now new paths let us know about people, situations and encounters that involve us more closely, making us all participants in this joyful and universal celebration.

We feel the desire to say thank you for inviting us, and very excited, we hug you.

Thanks Chuntianle, thanks Debrydelys, thanks to the book Sparkfire, thanks to everyone who will participate.

Chuntianle (New Power Art)

chuntianlec@gmail.com

Spring Impression

Airton Junior Gulart (Brazil)

Airton Junior Gulart is a musician and composer from the city of Santana do Livramento, in the state of Rio Grande do Sul, on the southern border with Uruguay.

He has been a music teacher since 2016. He is a cultural agent graduated from the Instituto Federal Sul-Riograndense. He is a history and geography teacher graduated from Universidade Paulista. He studied music education at UERGS. He annually promotes the Festa Nativa Canto a los Viejos (Native Festival of Canto a los Viejos). He is a representative musician from Rio Grande do Sul and organizer of the 1st Cultural and Musical Exchange in Santana do Livramento, RS. He is a speaker on "Cultural Identity". He currently works as a music therapist in the Mental Health lecture, together with his wife. In addition to native music, his repertoire includes Brazilian popular music.Ryan Lobo is a passionate musician whose love for creating and performing shines through in his original songs and cover tracks. With a deep connection to music, Ryan brings his heart and soul into each performance. He enjoys playing the piano and singing, allowing him to explore the beauty and emotions music can express.

Si j'ose dire (France)

It's like love

Songs have their mystery, they have their reasons for coming into the world but never say them... is it the unconscious that speaks, or God, or something else? Everyone will answer - or not - according to their convictions.

All life experiences are seeds that will germinate, perhaps, one day, in the form of songs. All the songwriter can do is take care of the earth, That is to say, cultivate his lucidity, enrich his knowledge, his culture... "Open your arms", Shane Mc Gowan said. And wait...very important, patience!

Of course, there are things: we take notes, we think, we try... but, for the most part, there's nothing to do, it either works or it doesn't: it's like love!

Afterwards, once the song is written, it's about performing it, making it come alive... If writing a song is not a job, performing it is. First, you have to master the technique: the singing, the instrument. This requires a long apprenticeship and daily practice. And then, and this is perhaps the most difficult, you have to find the state of mind you had when writing the song... you never find it exactly, there is always a bit of comedy in the interpretation, but you still have to live the song enough to be able to transmit it.And then, there too, there is an element of mystery, there are days with and days without...like love! The rest is up to the public to decide...

Chuntianle (New Power Art)

chuntianlec@gmail.com

Spring
Impression

171

Anderson GT (Peru)

Hello, I'm Anderson GT, since I was a child I have liked the Fingerstyle technique, this technique caught my attention when listening to Eiro Nareth, many told me that I could not reach that level, I studied Guitar in the United States and I have been practicing these techniques for almost 4 years and I have combined techniques from the United States and Japan and created instrumentals in my country Peru, thanks to that I went viral in a variety of countries, I was even congratulated by artists themselves such as (Dstance, Lúa, Manà, La banda deTOTO, Erick Elera, Etc) my most popular instrumental songs are (Ven - Erick Elera) (DTMF - Bad bunny) I am one more among the fingerstyle competitors from all over Latin America and I managed to impress many who did not believe that I would reach such a level, I do not know how far I will go, but with God's help everything will turn out well, lately the songs that I am releasing are going viral on spotify, despite all my effort, I feel that everything was worth it, but I finally achieved my goal.

Mika Melodies (USA)

Actions define one's success.

I have worked with amazing artists around the globe who would definitely agree with this philosophy.

To finish what we start requires discipline, determination, and persistence which are not easy to maintain. If your dream is important to you, then you should never give up midway when faced with adversities. The more you work on something the greater it becomes. But it is also important to not get distracted and lose track of the end goal.

The key is to stay committed, adapt to challenges, and keep moving forward. When you feel like giving up, remember why you started and how great it would feel to finally finish the task at hand. 2025 is the Year of the Snake and therefore the perfect year to complete all our unfinished tasks.

The ability to stay persistent and overcome setbacks separates those who succeed from those who give up.

(Mika Melodies is a singer/performer who plays multiple instruments. She was one of the top artists on the now-discontinued platform Sessions live and has performed for high-profile events at 5-star resorts. You can find her on almost all music streaming platforms. She goes by Mika Melodies Official on YouTube)

Chuntianle (New Power Art)

chuntianlec@gmail.com

Spring
Impression

CREATING WEALTH

**THE SECRET CODE OF SUCCESS IN
THE AI AGE & TIMELESS WISDOM**

A PERIODICAL FOR SOCIAL MEDIA
AND CONTENT CREATORS

A TRANSFORMATIONAL GUIDE TO BUILD BRAND,
AND INCREASE INCOME, INFLUENCE, AND IMPACT

Secret 18 Testimonial Matters

I immediately loved this brilliant idea of dedicating a thought to this particular year, so important in the Chinese zodiac, with all the following of emotions, sensations and hopes that this entails.

It was new enough for me too, an individual so modern and always looking for inner expansion. But if until recently the Chinese world seemed the only holder of this intriguing thought linked to this zodiacal year today this same intriguing thought conquers adepts and enthusiasts everywhere on our planet.

Many people hope, and among these people I myself wake up now with new hopes and new desires. The secret is to start knowing and experimenting with new paths that can even lead to radical changes in one's existence. Is this not, in fact, the year that also symbolizes inner reflection and creative impulses, encouraging change?

Personally I have always sought spirituality, as well as inner growth, because it is these dark forces, present within us, that can further stimulate us, and project us towards experiences that only a short time before did we not even believe possible. Here, I am like this, I want to believe that something more will come that will complete me.

And what could be better than starting this project together with Chuntianle? Isn't she the nice girl, the safe and pleasant source of inspiration for these suggestive scenarios that will arise for those who know how to dedicate themselves, body and soul, in search of a new rebirth?

The spark has now started and I often find myself talking to many friends, at the bar, at work, in film sets, or when I go shopping, and I ask them "what do you know and what the Chinese calendar represents for you, but above all what can this particular year be for you "?, and it's nice to find that many things were already filtered here in Europe, with parties, meetings between friends, debates and discussions with people who have origins and roots in very distant places, which I myself did in Radio locations. And so a nice range of communication possibilities opens up before our eyes.

Thinking about it, if I take inspiration from all the reflections and projects that this wonderful book offers, I think I have already started well in this splendid adventure, full of good hopes.

Debrydelys Deeberdeyn

Switzerland

It was the best, and just by seeing some more artists, I loved seeing how they develop in music and play good styles, it's great 10/10.

Anderson GT

Peru

ONE LAST MESSAGE

Congratulations on taking the leap towards improving yourself!

I'm really proud of your decision to dive into this book, learn from its strategies, real-life stories, cultures, fable, and fairy tales, and apply them to your business.

My mission with this book is to inspire you, to make you think differently, and to take action that drives positive change in your life.

I hope these pages have lit a fire in you, giving you the tools and motivation to chase your dreams and achieve more than you thought possible.

Your success is in your hands. No one can promise you a specific outcome, but the strategies in this book are simple yet powerful. They'll help you begin to pursue and accomplish any you desire.

If you want to explore success in music, creating multiple income streams, earning with AI, making money online, or engaging with a multicultural periodical, this book offers valuable insights to guide you. Again, congratulations! Best of luck on your journey to success.

Warm regards,

Chuntianle (YouTube/Instagram/Facebook: New Power Art)

> **"Set your life on fire. Seek those who fan your flames."**
> **–Persian Proverb**

Acknowledgments

To the many who've offered guidance, support, and inspiration through the years: your diverse impact on my life is deeply valued. While it's impossible to name each of you individually, your contributions haven't gone unnoticed. My heartfelt thanks to all; your influence is greatly appreciated.

Acknowledgments: I extend thanks to my friends for their guiding wisdom, for their unwavering support, and for their encouragement. To the countless others who've touched my life, your influence is deeply cherished, even if unlisted.

I apologize to those inadvertently left unmentioned. Your presence in my journey has been invaluable.

Lastly, to my family: your love has been my foundation. This book is a tribute to all who've shaped my path.

ABOUT Chuntianle (New Power Art)

Chuntianle (New Power Art) lives in the US. She is a loving, creative, inspirational spring impression music new power art leader and follows her core values: creativity, leadership, love, passion, and fairness. She helps artists to be in business to build wealth and brand. She loves spring, music, and art, and her work brings these traditions together. She is inspired by both Eastern and Western cultures. Influenced by the Impressionists and Renaissance masters, her Spring Impression music reflects the beauty of spring, combining Eastern charm with Western style.

She got calling, share message in Her book "**Creating Wealth**" that inspires you and allows you to gain inspiration and provides a transformational guide for success in music, personal growth, multiple income streams, etc.

Accomplishments:

Publication (Amazon #1 Bestseller Author)

- **Success in Music Made Simple**: A Transformational Guide for Success in Music, Personal Growth
- **Music Festival in AI Age**: A Transformational Guild for Success in Music Beyond Borders and Build Your Brand
- **Sparkfire - Art, Wealth and Success**: A Periodical Book for Emerging Social Media and Content Creators, a Revolutionary Guide to Increase your Influence, Income and Impact

- **Creating Wealth – The Secret Code of Success in The AI Age & Timeless Wisdom**: A Periodical for Social Media & Content Creators, a Transformational Guide to Build Your Brand and Increase your Influence, Income and Impact

- **International Spring Impression Music & Art Festival 2024, 2025:** Organizer, host, sponsor

- **International 4-Season Impression Art Event 2024**: Organizer, host, sponsor

- **Make Money Online Course, Chinese Class Online**

Numerous Spring Impression Music/Songs/Publication.

Oriental Culture Theme

- Original songs, such as Mother is Angel, Running Song, Girl in White, Little Spring Girl, Beautiful Spring Girl, and The Easter Birds, etc.

- Original theme music/songs for Chinese famous poems，ancient Chinese prose travel journal, etc.

- Piano theme series of famous Chinese masterpieces：Dream of Red Mansions Episode.

- Theme music for Liaozhai Zhiyi, sometimes shortened to Liaozhai, known in English as Strange Tales from a Chinese Studio.

- Theme music for Four Dreams of Linchuan, also called Yumingtang Si Meng (The Four Dreams of the Jade Tea Hall), by the famed Ming-dynasty dramatist Tang Xianzu (1550--1616).

- Theme: An excerpt from The 36 Stratagems (三十六计), classic collection of Chinese tactics offers strategic wisdom.

- Theme: The Hundred Family Surnames, an ancient Chinese primer on surnames.

- Theme: The twelve zodiac signs - A Timeless Reference.

Western Culture Theme

- Original piano theme music for famous painting and Spring Impression Music, such as： The Girl with a Pearl Earring by Vermeer, the mysterious masterpiece painting.

- Original piano theme music/Songs for Shakespeare's sonnets, plays. Such as:

  Sonnet 18: Shall I Compare Thee to a Summer's Day Song

  Sonnet 97 How like a Winter Hath My Absence Been

  Shakespeare's Romeo and Juliet - Come, Gentle Night

  Shakespeare Antony and Cleopatra, Love Story Piano

- Theme music: The Most Touching Love/Fairy tale in the World, such as "The Lady of the Camellias" Alexandre Dumas 《茶花女》, La Traviata, etc.

- Famous soprano art songs include 10 Italian songs, and other language, such French, German, English, Chinese, etc.

- Best poems turned into songs. Such as:

  "My Love is Like a Red Red Rose" by Robert Burns

  "She Walks in Beauty Song" by Lord Byron song

- Piano theme music: Wuthering Heights Emily Brontë, Chapters

YouTube.com/@NewPowerArt

Chuntianle plays piano, an Amazon #1Bestseller Author, a songwriter, and a soprano; she composed music/songs, she sings her own song too. Also, she is certified Project Management Professional (PMP), Certified Scrum Master (CSM), ITIL, a consultant (coach), an entrepreneur, She motivates people to improve their lives and strives to create a better community and a better world.